Nightsider

Sue Isle

First published in Australia in March 2011
by Twelfth Planet Press

www.twelfthplanetpress.com

Paper Dragons as © 2009 Sue Isle originally published in *Shiny* Issue 5
All other works © 2011 Sue Isle
Design and layout by Amanda Rainey
Typeset in Sabon MT Pro

All rights reserved. Without limiting the rights under copyright above, no part of this publication may be reproduced, stored in or introduced into a retrieval system, or transmitted in any form, or by any means (electronic, mechanical, photocopying, recording or otherwise), without the prior written permission of both the copyright owner and the above publisher of this book.

National Library of Australia Cataloguing-in-Publication entry

         Author: Isle, Sue.

         Title: Nightsiders : a twelve planets collection / by Sue Isle ; edited by Alisa Krasnostein.

         Edition: 1st ed.

         ISBN: 9780980827439 (pbk.)

         Series: Twelve planets.

         Target Audience: For young adults.

         Subjects: Perth (W.A.)--Fiction.

         Other Authors/Contributors:

                  Krasnostein, Alisa.

         Dewey Number: A823.3

For the Greens, who helped me to be aware of what could happen to our world. My stuff-ups and exaggerations are not their fault!

Also From Twelfth Planet Press

ANTHOLOGIES / COLLECTIONS:
2012, edited by Alisa Krasnostein and Ben Payne

New Ceres Nights, edited by Alisa Krasnostein and Tehani Wessely

A Book of Endings, by Deborah Biancotti

Glitter Rose, by Marianne de Pierres

Sprawl, edited by Alisa Krasnostein

NOVELLA SERIES:
Angel Rising, by Dirk Flinthart

Horn, by Peter M. Ball

Siren Beat, by Tansy Rayner Roberts / *Roadkill*, by Robert Shearman

Bleed, by Peter M. Ball

The Company Articles of Edward Teach, by Thoraiya Dyer / *The Angælien Apocalypse,* by Matthew Crulew

Above, by Stephanie Campisi / *Below*, by Ben Peek

WEBZINES:
Shiny Issues 1-6, edited by Alisa Krasnostein, Ben Payne, Tansy Rayner Roberts, Tehani Wessely

New Ceres Issues 1 and 2, edited by Alisa Krasnostein

Contents

Introduction 1

The Painted Girl 3

Nation of the Night 31

Paper Dragons 89

The Schoolteacher's Tale 113

Introduction

by Marianne de Pierres

The idea behind the Twelve Planets series is dear to my heart. As a writer of science fiction, and a female, I know how difficult it can be to bring any kind of attention to your work. When I heard Twelfth Planet Press were planning to showcase women SF writers who deserve better recognition I was truly honoured and delighted to be a part of it. Even more so to be able to introduce a writer with the talent and skill of Sue Isle. In the turn of a page your will enter the world of the Nightside, a dangerous future Australia; dry, hot and disintegrating. A place running to new rules but still riffing off old morality. A place where 'survival' is a character itself, lurking in shadows, stealing water and food.

In this wonderful body of work I hear echoes of two exceptional writers, Doris Lessing and Margo Lanagan. Sue Isles has Lessing's eye for compelling world building and Lanagan's hard hitting imagery, the combination of which creates a potent blend of fiction. And like Lanagan and Lessing, she does not shrink from portraying women in a very real way.

1

That said, her writing is uniquely hers, direct and honest and crowned by a deft ear for dialogue. As an Australian, particularly a Western Australian, I'm fascinated to see such familiar geography woven into her *imagineering* in a manner that retains its accessibility to lovers of speculative fiction all over the world. The reader encounters full immersion when they commit to Sue Isles' stories—absolutely the ONLY way to travel in fiction.

So turn the page now and be eager to read. But don't be casual … or the Nightside will take you.

The Painted Girl

The fire chased Kyra and Nerina into the city outskirts. Kyra didn't know quite where it was; somewhere behind them, a few hours distant, eating up the dead trees and the living as one, licking along the ground wherever there were fallen leaves or twigs or a discarded piece of clothing. The camp boss and his people were up ahead on the road with the rest of his motley crew following them.

The winds drove the fire and the dust. It didn't matter how much they covered up, the hot sandy wind always found its way beneath head coverings and down inside their clothes where it itched and made sores. Kyra wanted to take shelter until the dust settled and then go on into the city. Nerina didn't want to camp now and it was Nerina's say. Kyra had learned that when she was much smaller and Nerina's backhanded slap could send her stumbling and falling. She'd sit there and wail while Nerina walked on, ignoring her. Eventually she learned that Nerina would never stop for her.

Kyra was looking forward to seeing the city and new people. When she was in a good mood, Nerina told stories about her own childhood there which Kyra wasn't sure she believed. Of course, the system had been falling to pieces

3

even that long ago but Nerina had still been to a real school where a whole bunch of kids the same age sat in a room and got taught things. She'd tried to pass some of it on, at least to the extent of teaching Kyra to read but it hadn't taken all that well and Nerina lost patience with her too fast. 'You can read the road signs, you know how to find tucker and take care of yourself,' she'd say. 'That's the kind of school you need these days.'

The fire turned in another direction and the smoke haze lessened, meaning they were clear of it. Nerina had said that they were headed for the coast. These last few years they'd stayed inland, passing through the camps in the towns where you could stay three days no questions asked, but on the fourth day you were, as Nerina said, about as welcome as a dried dog turd. The camps blurred into a sameness of wary and hungry people, stinking of weariness and fear. The names rolled into one, Toodyay, Collie, Northam, York, Mandurah—though that was outlying city ruins and Nerina had only taken them around the outer fringe—towns deserted of livelihoods and visitors.

'Why did the people go away?' she had asked Nerina once and the woman had shrugged.

'There wasn't any rain and it got too dry.'

'So where did they go?'

'The planes and buses took them East.'

'Does it rain there?'

'That's enough stupid questions!'

Which was the way most such conversations ended.

***

The Painted Girl

The ground tipped downwards in front of Kyra's bare feet, into a dark maw. Nerina was apparently unconcerned. She pointed to a spear driven into the soil to the right of the cavern. A ragged white cloth hung from it like a spiritless flag. 'See that? That says this is safe ground. We can walk here, like we walked through the houses-land, so long as we don't stay. If we made a staying camp, took their food, then the people here would kill us.'

'They can kill us anyway if they want, can't they?'

'Can. Won't so long as we follow their law.'

'I don't want to go in there!'

'Too bad.' Nerina shrugged and walked into the dark entrance. Hungry, thirsty, tired, sick, scared. Didn't matter. She'd walk on and if Kyra wanted, she could stay behind and see how she liked aloneness. Too bad. The smell was the worst part. It told you there were alive things in there, watching you. Kyra pushed closer to Nerina until Nerina shoved her off. 'There's a light,' she said.

'I see it!'

It was a matchstick light, a tiny fire torch. As Kyra stared, an outline formed in the darkness. A person, sitting there below the light, back against the rocky wall, staring back at her and Nerina. Kyra couldn't hear anything beyond the light-circle, where an ambush party would wait. The person seemed truly alone. 'Are you okay?' Her voice came out shaky. Without meaning to, she'd halted, letting Nerina get a ways ahead of her. The person looked up. A girl her own age, at least Kyra thought so. Pale as a cave-fish that never saw the light but unlike such a fish, she did have eyes and seemed to be able to see. Kyra couldn't tell if she was wearing

5

any clothes, but her body was covered in a tracery of bright-coloured muds; white and ochre and yellows.

'Keep walking.' Her voice was husky as though she'd worn it out screaming. 'I'm in enough trouble.'

'You—you're being punished?'

'What, you never heard of trouble before?'

Nerina came back, several furious steps and grabbed Kyra's hand to tug her onwards. 'Don't you listen? I said we keep walking!'

The figure against the wall laughed. 'You're in safe, woman. There's only me. Your blood and bits can stay where they are. What's your name?'

Against Nerina's, 'No!' Kyra said it.

The painted girl coughed. It had a dry sound, as though no liquids had passed down her throat in quite some time. 'I'm Alicia.'

'You want to come with us?' Kyra fought the painful hold on her hand. 'You could come into the city.'

'No I couldn't. They don't let me.'

'She's a Drainer, you stupid child.' This time Nerina succeeded in tugging her on. 'Their punishments, their rewards, you leave alone!'

Alicia's husky laughter followed them but only for a little while.

They trekked out of the cavern of the Broken Line, which broke the city, Nerina told Kyra. Trains, which she'd seen only as wreckage, had run under the streets with a huge rumble like buried dragons. Kyra shivered at the thought of all those people. Since they had joined the flight from the

The Painted Girl

hall, Nerina smacked her arm. 'Pick up your feet!' The hall was larger than any inside place Kyra had ever been in. She couldn't see from end to end, there were too many stalls set up and people wandering around in the flickering lamplight. Every stall had several lanterns, more lights than she'd ever seen. The firelight didn't reach far and only people close by could be seen clearly; the more distant were vague shapes, dark against dark. In here, with all the bodies, it was stifling and she felt faint, ready to find a spot against a wall or under a table where she could sit and wait for Nerina to take care of whatever business she had here. She pulled at Nerina's hold but it was no good; she was hauled along like a sack of sand. Nerina halted in front of a trestle table, behind a couple of robed people talking to the stallholders. She glanced down at Kyra, frowning. This scared Kyra, who was not used to having Nerina look at her. She never did, unless she was furiously angry. 'Stand up straight,' she ordered. 'You stink. When did you last clean yourself?'

Kyra glared back but she felt too ill to launch into a shouting match. She wanted to tell Nerina she stank worse. She'd never seen Nerina take off her robe-like dress and the headcoverings were the same rags she'd worn as long as Kyra could remember. Nerina had taught her to scrub herself with sand but how could she do that here in the city? What sand there was was foul, with people and animals crapping in it. Her head hurt and so did her stomach. She hoped she hadn't caught some sickness; it would be easy to do among the crowds here and Nerina wouldn't let her slow down even if she was sick. She didn't spare herself either; Kyra had often seen her staggering along, pausing to vomit sideways before continuing on. Sometimes that was liquor but not always.

'I'm sick,' she said.

Nerina looked closely at her, gripping her head with one grimed hand while placing the other over Kyra's eyes, thumb and forefinger pulling the skin to make her keep her eyes open. 'No gunk and you're not snotty,' she diagnosed.

'Stomach hurts, head hurts. Thirsty.' Life with Nerina had taught her to reduce sentences to the most important things. If you were with the same person all the time for as long as you could remember, mostly you didn't need to talk.

'Hey,' called a voice and Nerina turned back. The people ahead of them were finished whatever it was and one of the seated men was gesturing. 'What've you got?'

They were definitely cityfolk, not outside traders. Their clothing didn't cover them the way hers and Nerina's did and they didn't even have any headcoverings. This stall was right up against the side, with maybe enough space behind it to be the people's living space while they were here at the market. There were two men and a woman.

'This,' Nerina said and tugged at her arm. 'Stand up straight, I told you!'

'How old?' the man who had spoken asked Nerina.

'Twelve—thirteen. I had her since she was maybe three—got her from some coast hideout. Never sick except for the usual kid stuff. Trained her good.'

'Thirteen?' The woman, who sat between the men, looked up from writing something. Kyra had been watching her; she rarely saw anyone write anything and then usually just

The Painted Girl

trail-marks. This was proper writing, the kind Nerina said she'd been taught to do in that school. 'Pre or post?'

'Pre.'

Why were they talking about her like this? What was that about Nerina having had her since she was three? Kyra looked confusedly at her. Your mother had you and then you were a baby, not three years old. Nerina was pushing at her now. 'Go sit over by the wall,' she said, indicating a spot just beyond the end of the trestle. It was what Kyra had wanted but now she was reluctant to move out of earshot, where Nerina clearly wanted her. She checked to be sure Kyra was obeying her before stepping closer to the table, leaning down to speak to the people. Kyra sank down the wall, resting her chin on her knees, arms around them, a protective huddle. She was still thirsty and her stomach ached but she could wait if she got to rest awhile.

She must have dozed. There was someone talking to her close up, not Nerina. This was unusual enough that Kyra immediately opened her eyes and tried to start back, except the red brick wall was there and she scraped against it. 'Easy,' said the woman. She was the one from the desk; short-haired and stocky, wearing a loose shirt which sun had faded to pink. The sleeves only came as far as her elbows. 'Can you stand up?' she went on. 'I need to have a look at you.'

'Why?' Kyra tried to see past her. There were more people around the trestle now and some in the space behind it with the sleeping rolls and packs. 'Where's Nerina?'

'We can talk after I look at you.'

'Where is she?' Panic sharpened Kyra's voice. It didn't matter that Nerina and she didn't like each other much; that

11

never mattered when you were on the bush trails. You just looked out for the other person because you needed them to look out for you, that was all.

'Never mind her.' The woman's voice, reasonably calm, was starting to quicken a little with impatience. 'I can't see anything of you in that tent you call a dress, so I need you to come around behind the table and take it off.'

'I'm not wearing anything under,' Kyra said.

'That doesn't matter.' She reached out and grasped Kyra's shoulders, easily lifting her to her feet. 'You hardly weigh a thing. Done a lot of walking?'

'Nothing but,' Kyra answered automatically. The woman let go of her shoulders before she would have struggled, watching her with calm attention. She gave a little nod in the direction she wanted Kyra to go and waited for her to do it. Given a small space and a moment to think, Kyra walked around the trestle table and stopped in front of the rolled-up bedding and packs. When she turned about, the woman was right there. 'Take off the dress,' she repeated, still patient but watchful.

Kyra did it and the woman examined her. Not the first she'd ever had; quite a few camps insisted that their doctor examine you before they let you through the gates but probably the first in the view of an entire community. Another trestle blocked off the space allotted to these people but no one sat at it. A lamp swung from a post propped against the unoccupied table. People wandered past and looked over at the skinny, indignant thirteen year old girl being checked out like a dubious horse. Then the woman said, 'Damn it.'

The Painted Girl

She was looking at Kyra's thigh as though it was some disappointing cut of meat. So she was skinny. Everyone was skinny unless they were rich and controlled a lot of people. This woman must be rich. She had excess flesh on just about every part of her body. It hung from her arms and throat. 'Simon, when's that tramp-woman due back?' she called.

'I told her end of the night,' one of the men replied. 'Why? Some problem?'

'Look here.'

He pushed his chair back, scraping it on the bare concrete floor and walked over, following the woman's gesture at Kyra and peering at her like faulty goods. 'Where?'

'Blood on her inner thigh.'

'Did you cut yourself?' Simon said to Kyra. 'Or is that your monthly?'

She shook her head, mystified and turned away from them to have a look herself. Blood streaked her inner thigh as though from some wound but there was nothing. She couldn't have forgotten hurting herself here and she hadn't taken her garments off for ages. The last time was Toodyay camp and a wash in the muddy river pools but there'd been nothing to hurt her there.

'Do you feel sick?' the woman asked, angry but seemingly at herself rather than Kyra.

'Yes. Sick here.' She indicated her gut. 'My head hurts.'

'How long? Were you sick before today?'

'No. Where's Nerina? She can tell you.'

'Don't mess around,' the woman said. 'She's menstruating. That customer's not going to want her.'

They shrugged at one another. 'Somebody'll come along

13

who's not so fussy,' Simon commented. His dark, disinterested eyes regarded Kyra for the briefest moment possible. He too carried extra weight.

'We'll need to move her right away.'

'Not worth the risk,' the other man said.

The woman appeared to come to some decision. 'Go see if you can find that woman, Simon. Get her to take the girl back until we set up another deal. Get dressed.' Her tone didn't change and it took a moment for Kyra to realise the last two words were directed at her, not the men. She quickly pulled the heavy cotton over her head, almost regretful as the extra heat layer settled against her skin. No one seemed to notice her then, so she sat against the wall, hoping there wasn't too much blood and her nausea would settle soon and that someone would eventually tell her what everyone was talking about.

The voices began again and she jumped, realising she'd dozed; a dreamless, shallow no-time which hadn't made her feel any better. '...no sign anywhere,' one of the male voices complained. 'Why don't we just let the girl go. She probably knows how to find her.'

'Because we agreed to keep her here until the woman came back,' the female voice answered heavily. 'It's a contract, remember.' Silence for a few moments and then the woman said, 'We'll keep her until the start of tomorrow night. There might be other offers.'

Kyra slumped all the way down to the stone floor, the closest to a cool place. No one noticed. She heard the scrape of bedding being pulled out and positioned but she didn't bother to look.

The Painted Girl

She woke, again, sensing it had been for a longer stretch, but she still didn't feel rested. Day-heat buzzed inside the hall, though the whole place was dim as a great cave. The distant doors looked closed. Between her and the trestle tables, the three bodies snored on their beds. Kyra looked, judged the distance and decided she could just manage to jump over them. She stood quietly, then very nearly squawked aloud as a hand closed about her bare ankle.

'Shsshh,' said a voice at her feet, young and faintly husky. 'I can take you somewhere but you gotta be quiet. Get back down.'

The smell, more than the voice, alerted her. Kyra turned and saw the paint-streaked face, hair lank and loose. 'Alicia?'

Alicia's grin showed a lot of white teeth. 'Hands and knees, follow under the tables,' she whispered, then let go of Kyra and suited action to words, scuttling like some little wild creature bound for refuge. Kyra did her best to follow, expecting any second to hear alerted adult voices and feel somebody grabbing her foot or hair. Alicia moved so quickly she made Kyra feel like some stiff old person, but she managed. When the painted girl crawled into a break in a wall that didn't look wide enough for a possum, Kyra held her breath and followed in right after her. It was wider than it looked. Sharp stones dug into her knees and she wanted to pause to brush them aside but Alicia wasn't stopping even though there was no shade outside the wall.

Kyra blinked, her eyes already drying. It was pretty stupid to walk around in full sun without a good reason. She could hardly see but Alicia came back and grabbed her arm, pulling her up and out of the hole in the wall. 'Nobody,' she

15

Nightsiders   Sue Isle

announced. 'What's wrong?'

'Can't see.' She blinked and rubbed her eyes but the glaring whiteness did not diminish. The sun struck the buildings around them and threw its heat back into the street. There was no breeze. Kyra looked automatically for a shady spot to go to but Alicia was still tugging at her arm. She was wearing only a large shawl of some bright mix of colours, which moved as she did, showing the tracery of paint on her body. Their gazes met; Kyra uneasily, Alicia with a slight frown as though she was trying to puzzle something out. Standing in the sun went against all Kyra's training. She wanted to crawl back inside where the strangers laired.

'She give you to the slavers,' Alicia said. 'I heard 'em. They were gonna sell you to one of them men likes little girls.' The Drainer girl sounded no more than mildly interested but then, what had she been doing close enough to listen? She seemed to be waiting for Kyra to do something. Kyra realised she in turn was waiting for a cuff on the side of the head and a terse order in Nerina's voice.

'You said you couldn't come into the city.' At once it sounded silly—who was she that Alicia owed her truth?

A shrug and grin. 'Not 'sposed. I don't let 'em see me.'

'Are you on your own?'

'Family down in the tunnels.' She stopped, leaving Kyra with the sense of more words choked off. 'I got to go. You come if you're coming.'

She couldn't go too far away. Nerina might changeabout and be sorry. Maybe she hadn't really meant to leave her? Alicia abruptly began to run and Kyra stumbled after her. Over hills of earth and rock in the burning white, around

16

The Painted Girl

standing buildings and the rare cityfolk who hadn't yet sought shelter, Alicia flickered, hard to see, harder to follow down crumbling streets. Then Alicia plunged downwards, out of sight and Kyra braked, at the top of a slope of gravel. Only dimly could she see the black entrance below, with the red earth and rock around it. Alicia's voice came huskily out of the blackness. 'Come on!'

It was cool inside the earth. Of course, a cave. Though built by humans, this was still a cave. Kyra turned about, enjoying the cooler air on her skin. The place smelled, of animals and humans, but she couldn't remember anywhere that didn't, except a brief wash of sea wind across her memory. She frowned but Alicia's voice, more impatient now, came from behind her. 'I said come on. My folk need to know about you.'

'I can't see yet,' Kyra pointed out, taking careful steps towards the voice. Alicia didn't answer but Kyra felt a sudden grip on her forearm and a tug.

'Ground's flat. This way.'

She was turned about within moments and had no idea whether they were moving further beneath the city or away from it. The smells were worse. Badly cured hides, maybe, and the warm-iron stink of blood. There was a bit more light, she realised, and in the way of it, knew that the light had been growing for a while. There was space again; dimly-visible walls and a roof several feet above her head and Alicia moving silently beside her. Holes in both sides of the tunnel let the light in, ragged entryways of small animals maybe. No exit for anything her size. The tunnel narrowed again and Alicia went ahead of her, confident and quick.

17

Wondering whether she was the fool Nerina had called her, Kyra followed.

Ahead, in what looked like a dead end, were people. Alicia turned, pushed a hand in her face and said, 'Don't move.' She went up to the people, who were settled about with bedding and seats and didn't bother to get up as the girls came in. Alicia came back to her, grabbed her arm again and pulled her unceremoniously forward until she stood within arm's reach of a woman who looked her over with the same sharply appraising gaze of the slaver. Her hair was rusty red, loose to her shoulders, and her face was very like Alicia's. *Other way round*, Kyra thought. She wore a loose, patterned garment; some kind of shawl that covered her upper body, well, some of it.

'Hello Kyra,' she said. 'Licia says you're in some trouble. Want to tell us what's going on?'

'I come in with Nerina,' Kyra answered in a low voice. She didn't want to tell them, didn't want to talk even, but when the camp boss asked you, you said. 'She gunna sell me to these people, they got some man wants a girl, only I started bleeding so they said that was wrong. And I run. You got to let Nerina cool when her head gets weird and so I asked Alicia if I could hang with her for a bit. That's it. I don't mean no trouble.'

The woman nodded her head a bit and Kyra understood; her account must have been enough like what Alicia had said.

'You plan to just go back to that woman that sold you?' she asked.

Kyra shrugged a little. 'I don't know what I plan.'

The Painted Girl

Someone struck a tinder and she smelled the hot rising of smoke and saw the spark. A little fire, already prepared, sprang alight and Kyra jumped in shock to see that there were maybe a dozen people here. The red-haired woman, the leader, was maybe the oldest but she counted another three women not much younger and two younger women or girls besides Alicia. Only three males were among them, casually looking her over. None was out of his twenties. The two younger women were both pregnant, more noticeable because none of the group was wearing much, none of the long loose clothes people wore outside in the sun.

'You stay here, you don't talk to people about us,' the woman—Alicia's mother?—said to Kyra. 'We know if you do and then you don't go to sleep more than twice before we find you, got it?'

Camp rules. Kyra felt surprised this woman thought she was that ignorant but she just nodded. The body stink of these folk was thick in her nostrils. You got used to any smell, any folk, given time, but she and Nerina'd been together and away from other groups a long time and it made her stomach uneasy. When the woman abruptly cuffed hard at the side of Alicia's head, she jumped but was not alarmed. This was usual.

'And you don't go up near them people without telling us! You could have led the lot on to us! You stay here today and you watch her. See?'

'I saw her come through travel tunnel to the city,' Alicia said, her young husky voice determined. 'She was with the crazy woman. I smell the crazy so I went up and found this one. Thought she'd be in the shit and she sure enough was.'

19

Nightsiders   Sue Isle

She grinned and so did the red-haired woman, even though her hand again swiped the air just above Alicia's head when Alicia ducked.

'You're not in charge yet, kid. Except of the camp, right now. We'll be back before sundown.'

'You all going?' Alicia asked forlornly. She glanced at the heavier of the two pregnant women. 'You going, Brit?'

The girl grinned, a white feral look. 'I'm playing bait,' she said. 'I take it real easy.'

'Enough games,' the leader ordered. 'Alan, you take your crew like we said, everyone else with me.'

Nine people moved as silently as one, past the girls into the bottleneck and away.

'Is that all your people?' Kyra asked.

'Yeah.' Alicia sighed. 'More soon, I guess, when Britni and Ione drop. Can't remember last time we had more'n one spawn around here, not since it was me and then the other one didn't make it.' She grinned and gestured Kyra forward. 'Pull up a seat. I'll get us something to eat. You thirsty?'

'Yeah,' Kyra said. It wasn't polite to ask for water; you had to wait until your hosts offered. Nerina had implied that 'Drainers' were some different kind of group and maybe that had to do with water custom. She watched Alicia go to the back of the dead end and reach for something hanging, a waterbottle. One of several, Kyra saw, all attached to long thongs which were tied to an outcrop of stone on the back wall. She also brought another hanging object, a bag of shiny leather, put her hand inside and brought out a handful of strips which she handed to her guest. 'It's cured,' she assured Kyra, who couldn't see the strips well enough to tell what

The Painted Girl

meat it was and was sniffing at it. She was less shy about the water, since her throat was quite dry, and reached eagerly for the bottle.

The iron-blood smell clung around the stopper and she hesitated despite her thirst. 'It's okay, it's plain water,' Alicia told her.

Kyra chewed some of the dried meat, finding it good but still unrecognisable. Maybe rabbit or even lamb; she'd never eaten much of that. Whoever did the curing had known their job. Before long she had eaten the entire handful and had another couple of gulps from the waterbottle. Her stomach still felt a bit queasy and she decided she had probably had enough to eat. She sat looking at Alicia, her painted designs slightly reflective. 'Is she your mum, the red-haired one?'

'Helen? Yeah. Britni and Ione are my sisters.'

'Is your dad with the group?'

Alicia laughed. 'No way. Helen doesn't let old guys stay, she says they boss if they do. We got a couple now, for Britni and Ione, but Helen says if we pick too many from outside us, we'd lose control.'

Kyra let the words slide over without really thinking too hard about their meaning. A full stomach made her much happier and able to face the world. She wondered whether Nerina had come back to her senses yet. She envied Alicia her family about her. She'd never had any family. No, that was wrong. She must have. Nerina had said something about taking her from people. Funny that she couldn't remember any of it but she could smell the sea when she thought about it. She yawned.

'You need to sleep?' Alicia asked.

Nightsiders   Sue Isle

'Yeah. I usually do, in the day.'

Alicia laughed. 'Not me but we don't have anything else to do and I was out real early for us, looking for you.'

'Why?' Kyra asked curiously.

'I dunno. You talked to me when you come through, that was weird and I got to wondering where you'd gone. No kids in the group my age either.'

They settled haphazardly on the bedding and Kyra felt weariness sink into her body. It felt like days since she'd got any real sleep. She wondered, just before she fell asleep, why Alicia's people went out in the day. There wouldn't be anyone around and no animals awake either to be hunted.

She woke quickly, as she always did, but hearing voices around her as though they'd been talking for awhile. Camp talk, mostly; pass this, geez, this meat is tough, where did you find those cans? They'd found a cache, she gathered, taken its contents. Which was against any camp rules she knew but maybe city was different.

It was easy talk, casual, including Alicia, because Kyra heard her voice asking questions. She decided it was time she woke up. She drew her breath in, stretched and opened her eyes. They were all around, watching her. It was dark, no light coming in from outside but someone had lit a lantern and placed it on the ground with the various containers of food and drink. A regular cave picnic but Kyra didn't want to eat, even though her stomach felt empty.

'You can't go out now,' the red-haired woman said. 'Somebody might see you coming out and get curious.'

A jolt of nervousness rattled her. She didn't like the stares. One of the women was eating a dried strip of meat

22

The Painted Girl

but she never took her gaze off Kyra. *They all look alike*, she thought randomly. Not quite the same; there were differences in hair shadings and distinctions of face and body but more the same than herself and Nerina, for example. Her only example. This was family sitting in the near darkness, sharing food and talk and she was on the out. Even Alicia looked wary and Kyra wondered whether she'd been talked to about bringing Kyra in.

'Okay,' she said, after a too-long pause.

'You got more family than the crazy woman?'

'I did. Well, she said I did. The people she took me from.'

'How long ago was that?' Helen asked.

'Maybe ten years.'

'Dry bones then,' Helen said, not unsympathetically. 'Wasn't the city, was it?'

'No. Some place near a beach. I don't remember.'

They all laughed then and Kyra understood; she was the mealtime entertainment. She didn't mind. It was the way of the camps.

'Nobody stays in one place that long,' Helen told her. 'You know that, don't you?' Kyra nodded. 'We could find the place and never know it.'

'Maybe they went east.'

'If they did you got no hope. You'd never get there and if you did, they'd stow you in a transie camp and make you work for 'em. I tell you what, girl. You come with us, tomorrow, see how you do. Maybe you can work in with us, you're young enough and you're tough or you wouldn't still be alive. We could be your family. You think on it.'

***

Nightsiders   Sue Isle

The world burned.

Helen gave Kyra a headscarf of some light, silky material but the sun still struck at her. She wondered at the way the rest of the troop moved unprotected, some even bare-headed, through the blazing day. They had separated, in what Kyra thought was custom, into groups of three or four, leaving at intervals for different areas of the sand-drowned city. She was with Helen, Alicia, Ione and one of the men, whose name she had not heard. Unlike them, she needed to stop frequently and drink from the flask Alicia had given her. On these occasions, she saw Helen watching her thoughtfully, and she struggled to keep up.

The Nightsiders, the two thousand-some denizens of the city, were all in their lairs, leaving the city open and silent save for the Drainers. Even if some were wakeful, Alicia told Kyra, they would never come out and would only watch from the shade of a half-crumbling building or lean-to. *Don't want to attract our attention*, she said gleefully.

'What would you do?' Kyra asked her, half-whispering.

Helen heard them. 'Usually nothing,' she said, gazing at Kyra. 'Depends what we need. If we're hungry.'

'But if they don't hurt you...'

'They would if they dared. We talk to a few of 'em, a little, but mostly we can't trust them.'

The troop roamed around the open ground. It was paved with pinkish brick and framed by buildings which the Nightsiders were trying to restore. Helen pointed out the art school. It had canvas sheeting on the front and people lived in it now. Opposite, above the amphitheatre, was a library and an art gallery—a place where people had once

The Painted Girl

set out pictures so you could look at them. Helen shrugged at the blank expressions of her daughter and Kyra. They moved outward, into the narrower streets where buildings were several storeys high but shaky-dangerous; if you went into them you could bring them crumbling down on you. People lived there anyway. There were camps everywhere; sometimes they saw people, mostly sleeping, all unaware of the group moving among them. Helen and her people were bright ghosts of the daytime, moving quietly and gone before anyone could properly wake.

Then they found Nerina's camp.

It was like nothing had happened. She'd made a lean-to against a wall, like usual, and was sleeping up against it in the best shade she could, with her pack between her and the wall. A small fireplace with ashes carefully put out, a battered pot beside it. Everything was battered, held together with bits of wire, smelling of age and dust and not washing. Kyra's pack was there too but dumped on the ground by the fireplace, unguarded. She wouldn't have been surprised to turn around and find the four people gone but they moved in to surround the sleeping Nerina. She woke with an inarticulate growl and swung an arm at the nearest.

Helen closed her hand around Nerina's arm, held her awkwardly, half-up, half still in a heap. 'We have some questions,' she said.

Nerina's eyes flickered away, found Kyra at the back of the group, head covered and face shaded. 'Get away,' she snarled. 'Got nothing you lot want and I've had enough of this kid. Can't even sell it.'

'Where did you get the child?' Helen asked, cool, calm.

Nightsiders   Sue Isle

She let go of Nerina, who scrambled awkwardly to her feet and stepped away.

'Dunno. Somewhere along the coast, long time ago. Probably not even there anymore. Little tribe, all out looking for food, left their kids in the hide. Dunno why, didn't want one much but oldest kid come at me, boy ten, eleven years, tried to cut me. Yelling murder. I knocked him on the head, hard and out. This one, real small, screaming, had to shut it up, take it with me. Then couldn't fucking well get rid of it!'

'Where were the kids?' said Helen.

Through the following ramble into the past and forward to the present, circling confusedly around Helen's question, fielding a patchy memory and patchier time-sense, the past emerged. Kyra began to understand Helen's tactics. She never left her question, no matter where Nerina's words wandered, no matter how indifferent or hurtful. By simple repetition, 'Was it here? Further here? Were there sand dunes? Trees by the beach? How far did you travel that day? Where did you stop?' a picture was slowly forming of Kyra's last ten, meandering, hungry years.

Kyra's head ached with heat. She wanted another drink and to move into the shade. The four Drainers didn't seem to care or even to be uncomfortable. Finally Helen shrugged and turned away. The questioning had not ended anywhere useful that Kyra could mark. Perhaps Helen had just given up on Nerina, who had turned her back and was gathering up her camp into a single swag. Helen touched Kyra's shoulder and indicated southwards. 'Follow if you want,' she said and with that the four were gone, swift as sunlight shadows.

Kyra stood alone. She had to remind herself not to help,

The Painted Girl

that she was not a part of this camp, of this tiny tribe of two people, any more.

'I guess you didn't want to kill me,' she said. 'But didn't you…' From nowhere she recognised came an upheaval of misery, a wish to just start bawling and let the wasteful tears flow. 'Didn't you ever want me there? I helped you. Times you were sick, times I got the food, stood watch.'

Nerina didn't stop her preparations but a few moments later she spoke. 'Handy to have a second, once you got past the shitting and screaming. Kid's handy. Don't want another woman in the camp, no way.' She swung the swag awkwardly, without Kyra's hands steadying it, settled it on her back. 'Don't you follow. I ain't gonna feed you.'

Kyra stood there a long time, well after Nerina was out of sight beyond the buildings and the rubble, until the burning of her skin told her that for her life, she had to get out of the sun.

Not far away, the Drainers were waiting.

'Nerina couldn't relate to adults,' Helen said, as though continuing a conversation that had begun some time ago. 'Not to people at all, really, though she could control a young child. The moment you showed any sign of free will, she panicked.'

'Panicked!' Kyra burst out. That hadn't looked like panic. It had looked more like Nerina brushing bird droppings off her arm.

'She may have decided to sell you earlier or only when she came into the city and found out about the traders' market. That's impossible to tell. But I do now have a fair idea of the area where she found you.'

Kyra stared at her. Alicia was grinning as though in possession of a juicy secret. 'I got nothing to trade you,' Kyra said. In her world, in Nerina's, no one did anything for nothing. If you did, the sun sucked your bones. These folk, these eerie Drainers who walked unharmed in the sun, why would they do her a favour for nothing? She wasn't like them. This time in the sun had drained her and she longed to rest, like some old gran no longer able to travel with her camp.

'You do, in fact,' Helen said. 'There are people in the city who pay for information such as that I dragged out of that miserable tramp-woman. They want to make contact with small groups such as your birth tribe who hide themselves away from the city and probably from other folk as well. They say the only chance for our ultimate survival is to bring all such tribe-fragments together here.' She waved a hand around in a circle to indicate the dry, dusty street.

'But you said they were probably bones.'

'They may be. From what Nerina said, though, they were fairly well set up. It was pure bad luck that the adults were too far away to hear you or the other children when you called for help. There didn't seem to be any main track nearby; Nerina simply meandered and found you by accident rather than cunning. It's not likely she killed the boy by hitting him once with a stick, though it's possible. No, I think they are still there and still keeping themselves hidden.'

Kyra looked at them uncertainly.

'You still believe we want to kill them and drink their blood?' Helen was mocking her now and there was nothing friendly about it. 'You think that's why we roam by day?'

The Painted Girl

'You—you can do things people don't—the sun doesn't hurt you and you don't get as thirsty…'

'We're the result of a freak mutation,' Helen said precisely. 'We maintain it by inbreeding to a careful schedule—yes, I know you don't understand me, child. I suppose I shouldn't blame you. I used to teach biology, you know, not that that will make any sort of sense to you. We do hunt folk—and take their food stash, their swags—because it's them or us. Yes, we scavenge bodies, if hunger is enough. Not often because to eat your own kind contains its own threat in the form of various unpleasant diseases. So you've got that choice now, child. We'll try to find your folk and we'll talk to those people I mentioned. No promises. If you have any knowledge to trade, that's what you can use. If you don't want to stay with us, there's somewhere else I can take you, to people who will look after you. They take children with no tribe and they don't harm them.'

The sun hurt, even though it was almost set and the shadows lengthened. Alicia fidgeted beside Helen, watching Kyra but saying nothing.

'I want to know,' Kyra said slowly and how strange it felt, declaring her own intent. 'I want to know whether my people are bones.'

'Then we'll find out,' Helen answered her.

When Kyra began to walk beside them, it felt like going home.

Nation of the Night

When I was maybe seventeen, I went to see Prof Daniel for help with a problem. Not unusual, that was for sure, but this problem was my whole life.

Even writing the words is hard.

I woke up with a gut-ache that day, not long before sunset, and found that I was bleeding from inside. The way girls do when they become women. The problem wasn't that I didn't know what had happened to me. The problem was that I'm not a girl. Not in my head.

Somebody told me once that Daniel used to teach at the last university but he'd gone in one of the first cutback purges. Whether that was true or not, the Prof knew something about a lot of things and had books about the rest. We'd met when I was just a kid and I'd never told him about me, but figured he would neither be shocked nor horrified. I'd hoped I'd be able to find the information in one of his books and not have to say.

I was sharing quarters with the street acting troupe at that time, in the PICA building, fairly close to the Prof's place on Stirling Street. So not long after it got dark and everyone was up and about, I headed outside. I jogged

31

through the early night, which was still as hot and thick as a fur blanket.

At Daniel's building, I opened the door quietly and called inside, 'Hi, this is Ash. Okay to come in?' There was nothing you could call security, but people were protective of their space. When there was no answer, I went in and climbed the stairs, glad to meet no one on them, until I got to the top floor. Daniel had the two useable rooms for himself and any guests who happened along.

'Hey, Ash,' his voice reached me, after a few moments which made me sure he'd just woken. 'Come on in.'

The place was so musty that the first thing I did was sneeze. I wondered how long it had been since Daniel had even opened the door. The room had been swept, at least, because I could see floorboards. It was crowded with storage boxes but they were all lined along the walls and filled with stuff. The big table where he taught was clear except for some books and Daniel himself was standing in the doorway to the other room, which served him as both lair and library.

'You're not due for a lesson, are you?' he asked, mildly enough for somebody who'd been rousted out of bed.

'No, sorry, I forgot it was early. Just wanted to look something up.'

'It must be important.' Daniel moved absently towards one of the big water barrels, tapped it and turned the spigot, but only a trickle came out.

'Hey, when did you run out?'

'Not long, don't worry. It's just annoying when I forget and go for a drink.'

Nation of the Night

The books could wait. 'I'll get you a couple of buckets,' I said. 'If I can round up some kids, we'll fill it but it's not the usual time and I don't have any tokens on me. Anything else you need?'

'The water will do for now,' he said. He sounded a bit hoarse, like he wasn't well, and I looked at him carefully. There was only the one source of light, the lantern over on top of one of the storage boxes, but we were all used to seeing in the almost-dark. I stared at the Professor, taking in his paleness as though for the first time. Like all of us, Daniel wore as little as he could get away with, meaning a pair of shorts. He had always been skinny, too, and wore a beard which was three parts grey, though he wouldn't admit to being more than fifty. He knew too much history to only be fifty.

'Don't stare like that, Ash, it makes you look like a zombie,' he told me. 'I tell you what, you get the water and I'll make a start on finding the info you wanted. I might even know it. What obscure material are you looking for these days?'

'Uh,' I said. 'It's kind of complicated. It's okay, I'll tell you when I get back.' Or I'd find a good lie. One of the two.

The street outside was filling with people setting out on their business of the night. Though there are only a couple of thousand of us, according to the people who actually bother to do the counting, we tended to live fairly close together around the CBD. As old lady Wakey used to tell us as kids, it was all we could cope with anyway. We built gardens and farms and protected them from the heat, took brackish

33

Nightsiders   Sue Isle

water from the river and desalinated it using a little plant,
nothing like the huge concrete water-factories that are now
just bombed out ruins.

I talked to people as I went, if anyone recognised me or if
I recognised them. It was a steady stream of, 'hi, yeah, good,
getting water, how about you?' person by person, through
parts of the city that weren't strictly mine to walk in. My
arms and back and everywhere else were aching fit to die
when I got the bucket up the stairs. My gut was still aching
too. I wished the desal had been set up this side of the river
instead of kilometres away. There was a small community
who lived around it and traded in the water, but it wasn't
that much help to those of us whose territory was here. We
didn't often have stuff to trade to them.

'Thanks, Ash,' Daniel said. 'Did you still want to look up
your project or are you too tired?'

There was my out, but like an idiot I didn't want him to
think I was anything so wussy as tired. I went into the other
room with a candle, careful to keep it away from the books.

Daniel's library was packed into bookshelves occupying
the room's three main walls. To one side of the door sat his
bed and a small chest of drawers which held a few clothes. He
didn't have any sunscreen gear, which made me wonder again
just how many times he'd left this place since moving in.

The windows were boarded up. No pretence with
curtains. The sun didn't get in here, period. Nor were the
books supposed to be exposed to direct sunlight, i.e. you
could take them to the main table but if you took them
outside, they would be rebound in your hide. I knew Daniel's
library well enough to know he had a few medical texts,

34

Nation of the Night

some basic enough for me to follow. I had to admit that was pretty basic. I knew human biology had once been a subject taught to kids but not too much more.

The main room was quiet except for the brushing of Daniel's feet on the faded boards. I stood with my back to the connecting door, a book half pulled out from the shelf.

'You want to tell me?' he asked.

'No,' I said.

'You want to know something for you or something for somebody else?'

I took a couple of steps closer to look at the book's cover. *Midwifery*, it read. Not exactly helpful.

'For me,' I said.

'Not planning a new career?'

'No way,' I said and put the book back.

'How old are you now?' he asked, as though idly curious.

'Between sixteen and seventeen, I think,' I said.

'That was a child once,' Daniel mused. 'Historically, in some countries a boy or girl past puberty was an adult, but in modern times they were turned into children, because the societies they lived in didn't know what to do with them. They made them useless until they were almost fully grown…'

'Get off me,' I said, knowing it was rude, knowing he'd just prodded me to see if I'd yelp.

'Not on you,' Daniel said serenely. 'But none of the books there have Twelve Easy Answers to Teenage Angst.'

'You were a professor of mathematics, not—not of…'

'Psychology, I think you're trying to say,' he cut me off. 'It wouldn't hurt you to get a bit more education, you know. I

35

Nightsiders   Sue Isle

can guess, pretty well, that any problem you want help with is not covered in those books in any way that would help. But you don't have to listen. Crash here tonight and you can read anything you like tomorrow when there's more light. I owe you that. You can eat here, I don't suppose you got a chance to grab anything yourself? No?'

He backed off, to my relief, and went out to see about food. I touched one or two more books and then went out to the main room. Daniel looked older in the scanty light from the lantern, chopping vegetables. He handed me a carrot and I bit into it; tough, still earthy, but food. I sat down in one of the mismatched chairs, chomping steadily.

'I don't know if you know,' I blurted. 'About me.'

'I know there are things in your past that you might not want to talk about, but you could say that of any of us, child or adult, who stayed behind here,' Daniel said, not turning. 'Would it be easier for you to talk to Ellen Wakeling, perhaps?'

'Talk to old lady Wakey?' I said, horrified. It was funny, I might be nearly grown up, the way he was saying, but the moment he said her name, I was eight again, shrinking into the floor in front of the teacher, who had just caught me at some crime or other. I hadn't spent much time around the school since I was fourteen and had come to Daniel to learn maths. The adults around me agreed. They couldn't spare their personal time every day to frogmarch me or any other reluctant kid into school.

'Some things are better from a woman,' Daniel said carefully, so carefully I was suddenly sure he knew and felt the

36

Nation of the Night

sickness in my gut. 'She's also used to phrasing complicated things so that young people can understand.'

'Why better from a woman?' My voice went high and screechy.

'I don't know. People always say that, but it always reminds me, for some perverse reason, of the Amerindian tradition of having women torture the tribe's prisoners. Kipling wrote about it in his poem, "The Female of the Species":

> *When early Jesuit fathers preached to Hurons
> and Choctaws
> They prayed to be delivered from the vengeance
> of the squaws
> T'was the women, not the warriors, made those
> stark enthusiasts pale
> For the female of the species is more deadly than
> the male!'*

'Yeah. Cute,' I said without enthusiasm. 'Sounds just like old lady—I mean, Miss Wakeling's thing.'

He turned around and handed me a bowl of chopped vegetables. 'Try to eat that like a civilised being. Water?'

'Thanks.'

He poured us each a mug, careful not to spill any. It was the last of his supply. He hadn't had time yet to boil what I had brought.

'We aren't civilized, are we, Prof? I mean, we're just what scuttles around in the ruins.'

'Is that a Tom Roper quote?' I nodded. Tom was the chief of the street actors group and one of my caretakers when I was small. 'Well, partly he's right, but it's not just material

37

things that make a person civilized. It comes from inside him. If you find someone hurt and you help him, give him water and shelter, then you're a civilised being, aren't you, whether or not you have reliable electricity—we're working on restoring it to this building, by the way—or even a government.'

'There are some police in the city,' I said, wondering if I was being stupid, but he nodded emphatically.

'They volunteered to stay here, to do their best to take care of us. Of course, it isn't their responsibility to keep us civilised, only to try to stop us killing or robbing one another, and they can do so only in the small circle of territory which was once the heart of the city. But their presence is a mark of civilisation, you're quite right. I'm sure they'd advise you if you've got a, um, criminal difficulty…'

I had to laugh. 'That's fine, Daniel. I don't have a guilty conscience about a break and enter.'

'It's strange what stays in the language even after useful application is gone, but thank you, Ash. That relieves me no end.' He muttered something about 'moral shifts' and ate most of a potato before speaking again. 'So?' He didn't say anything else and I understood that we had shifted back to the basic question.

'I'm bleeding,' I said. 'I need to know how to stop it.'

He looked at my face then, neither smiling nor frowning. My tone must have tipped him off that I wasn't talking about some injury, but I wouldn't have danced around like a possum on hot bitumen if it was only that. 'I see,' he said.

'Did you know?'

Nation of the Night

'Not at first. I worked it out. It took some time, because you aren't hiding. You aren't gameplaying.'

'Why would I do that?'

'Why indeed?' He looked away from me. 'The short answer is you can't stop it, Ash. There's medication that will, or an operation that will, but we don't have those things here. You'd have to go to one of the eastern cities. That is, if the doctors there will agree to help you. If it helps, you're lucky, you know. Sixteen to seventeen is very late to start menstruation. Possibly malnutrition is a factor. Your lifestlye.' He scraped the last scraps from his bowl and ate them slowly. 'I do know someone here whom you could talk to. If he gave you his support, there's a better chance the doctors in the east would listen enough for that. Listen, Ash, I am reading your rather muddy words correctly, aren't I? You're a girl, here.' He tapped his chest, waved vaguely downwards. 'But you are a boy. That is what you're saying?'

I wanted to run and hide or jump out of the window, never mind we were five floors up. 'Yeah,' I said. My mouth had dried up and I took a gulp of the water and immediately started coughing.

'Don't you dare spit that out,' Daniel informed me direly. I coughed some more but finally managed to swallow the water back down. 'Good boy,' Daniel said, when we were both sure it would stay. 'Finish your food like a civilised man.'

***

I thought he'd forgotten the whole thing. I almost hoped he had, but a few nights later when I went to see Daniel, he had company. I started to back out but he said, 'No, that's all right, I was going to send somebody to find you, in fact. Come in, Ash.' I did, beginning to suspect a set up, but I could always run away.

The stranger sat at the study table, a mug of water before him. I guessed he was maybe fifty, which made him oldfolk in our world. That meant he had some skill people wanted.

'This is Dr Mitchell,' Daniel said, making a gesture which was halfway between waving and swiping at a fly. The man nodded briefly at me, seeming casual, but the way he looked at me was pretty intense. I was used to people who only met your eyes for a moment and then looked somewhere else, the way that was polite to people my age and maybe a few years more than that. This guy had grown up in Daniel's generation. He was even wearing a shirt with long sleeves, though no jacket and tie, the way men did in pictures from before the Evac. I figured he was probably sorry about that now, after walking from Wherever—he couldn't live nearby—and then up all our stairs. There were dark patches of sweat under his arms.

'I thought I knew the doctors in town,' I said, already guessing what this guy might be, given my conversation with Daniel of a few nights ago.

'I'm not a medical doctor,' he said. 'I'm a psychologist, what you might call a counsellor.' I gave that a few beats and then he added into the silence, 'When there was a thriving city here, I would have been the person your doctor sent you to see when you said you wanted sex reassignment surgery.

Nation of the Night

I'd talk to you and find out if you were genuinely gender-dysphoric and then whether you were stable enough to go through the entire procedure when you were eighteen. Do you understand what I've just said to you?'

I felt a flash of anger then. Okay, so I was a lot younger than him and I lived in the ruins, but that did not mean I was stupid. What did this idiot mean by talking to me this way? Then I saw his look. Not patronising or mocking, but almost eager, waiting for me to explode at him.

'Why do I have to see you now then?'

'Because you won't get clearance by the doctors over East if you don't,' he said, quietly now. 'Yes, I know you're too young, but I also know it's going to take you some time to arrange the journey and you also need to prepare yourself, more than you might think.'

I shrugged, like it didn't matter. I couldn't quite get it clear in my head what the doctors could do anyway. Daniel's books were nowhere near specific enough and he didn't know. Sure, I knew I didn't look right, for a boy, when you got to the basic equipment.

'Okay. We can talk.'

'Not here,' he said. 'Come to my rooms and we'll talk there.'

We didn't only talk. Mitchell gave me pills which he said were part of the process. He'd obtained them from his colleagues in Melbourne. I was a bit guilty, figuring he must have been working overtime talking to those colleagues, and wished there was something real I could do to help. When I said that, he smiled a little.

'The Professor has taken care of that. I owe him ... well,

41

Nightsiders   Sue Isle

sufficient that helping you doesn't quite clear my debt, in my opinion.'

We were in his central city office, the fan at least shifting the heavy twilight air around the room. He lived here as well, this apartment above a former shop contained sleeping quarters and kitchen, plus the room he used to see clients. It was bare and shabby, like everywhere in the city, but very clean. I jiggled the little bottle of pills in my hand. 'So what will they do?'

'They'll make you look more male,' Mitchell said. 'You'll also feel more aggressive, so watch that. If anybody annoys you, give him a second chance before you decide he doesn't need to live.'

I grinned at that. In my world, you had to convince people it wasn't worth their while to hassle you, if you wanted to grow up. Mitchell frowned at me, so I made a conscious effort to look serious. 'Sorry, doctor.'

Mitchell still didn't seem all that certain about my maturity, but he did write to people he knew in the medical profession in the east and put his case for me being allowed to have the sex reassignment surgery. We'd decided to tell them I was now eighteen, since nobody knew for sure. When the reply made it back, a couple of months after that, Mitchell sent a message for me to come in to read it.

Even in print, I wasn't sure I liked his surgeon friend, even though she was inviting me to come to the Melbourne hospital where she worked to have the sex-change surgery, so long as I passed their psych test as well.

'We need to be sure this young woman is fully mature enough to make this decision,' she wrote.

Nation of the Night

'Young—why's she dancing around this?'

'She's worried about being sued by your parents,' Mitchell told me.

'What parents? Didn't you tell them about me?'

'Of course, but they know about medicine, not about the way things are here.'

That made sense, I supposed, but I could hardly bring myself to read the printed words, to accept that this Dr Bornstein was really talking about me when she wrote, 'this young woman'.

Mitchell shrugged, waving the letter in a fanning motion. His room was hot and airless. The erratic electricity hadn't been working for a few days and the local residents hadn't found anyone to fix it. Now he said, 'You could come to an arrangement with the next camel train, you know. Might end up quicker than waiting for a truck.'

'More chance of being robbed, skinned and dumped in the desert to die,' I muttered.

'You know that's an urban myth.'

'If it's a myth, why do I know at least four people who signed on to travel with them who never came home?'

'I don't know,' the psychologist said, dismissing me. 'She's said here to come ASAP. So however you arrange your travel, do it.'

I got two truck rides. The first took me through a bare and dry landscape—the Nullarbor plain—which the driver said was as empty as it had always been. We unloaded in Adelaide, which also seemed mostly deserted and hot, though cooler than home.

Nightsiders   Sue Isle

The ride to Melbourne left its depot barely an hour after we pulled in that afternoon so I had hardly enough time to say goodbye to the first driver before I had to climb into the second cab. We drove for another eighteen hours, during which time my job was to chat and recite and do any damn thing to make sure Jamil, the driver, didn't fall asleep, same as I'd done for the first guy. There were little towns along our way, at least houses, but we didn't see any people, not even at the roadhouse where the precious fuel was stored. One of the truck company's people was meant to live there, armed with a rifle, to protect it, but there wasn't so much as the glint on a barrel while Jamil filled the tank.

I fell asleep eventually, about three hours from our destination, so I didn't see the huge city taking shape around me. Instead, I woke to Jamil poking me in the ribs and opened my eyes to looming, built-up greyness. Ellen Wakeling had told me that, before civilisation came crashing down, Melbourne had been a prosperous city perhaps four times the size of Perth, vibrant and creative and industrious. The truth of it was like a blow to my head. All the people! I'd never seen such crowds, filling the streets, even in the road, visible in the building fronts. The truck lumbered over a bridge spanning a narrow brown river, the water so high it lapped over the stone-covered banks. I glanced up, trying to see the sky above the tall buildings. It was overcast with cloud, making it difficult to see clearly in the muted light.

The road before us was wider than I was used to, with metal tracks running down its centre. Had they once had trains here, mixed up with their other vehicles? I decided to keep my dumb questions to myself as much as I could.

44

Nation of the Night

The buildings were mostly intact, far more so than home, but they didn't look prosperous either. Huge windows which had probably had glass once were now covered with tarpaulins or wooden frames. Decades of neglect added dirt and shabbiness.

'This area used to be some fancy tourist precinct,' Jamil announced, in his tour guide role. 'Before the Evac, anyway. When all those people come and the fuel got so scarce, they had to put 'em somewhere.'

'I used to think only Perth got hit by the Evac, but looks like this place did too. I wonder why they were able to keep Melbourne and the other eastern cities going and not us?'

'Hah,' Jamil snorted. 'All these cities are way closer to each other than yours to any of them. There's a network linking Adelaide and Melbourne and Sydney, Canberra and Brisbane. We all use it but we only go to Perth once in a long while. Perth's too far from everything. If the rest of the cities had to keep Perth going, it would drag everyone down. You're lucky. Whatever you're here for, it's your wedge in. They can't treat you as a refugee with that medical pass...'

'It's just a letter.'

'It gets you in,' Jamil insisted. 'Like me, right? I got in because I got a letter from my uncle Abdullah with the trucking company, promising me a job. I not got that, they march me out of the city and say, "Keep walking". The Evac was a once-off. My ma, she don't want to leave...'

'I'm going home after,' I said.

Jamil spat out of the window. 'You're mad. You got to look around first.' He said it with perfect amiability. 'The depot's back that way, but I'll drop you where you got to go.

45

Nightsiders   Sue Isle

There haven't been any buses or trams since last year. You got somewhere to stay?'

'I'll find somewhere. First I've got to get to the hospital—address is here—and find this doctor.'

Jamil took the letter, read briefly and gave it back. 'That's the reffo hospital on the South Wharf. You try to sleep on the streets around there, the cops move you on.'

I murmured denial of any such plan, not wanting to annoy Jamil in the last few minutes of our acquaintance, but the truth was there wasn't much choice. I had to find the hospital and get directions as to where to show up when. Beyond that, I would join the shadow people and hope to stay alive until it was time for me to leave. A stranger rides into town, but no one asks the town if they want him or the changes he'll bring.

Jamil pulled over, ignoring the startled pedestrians who scrambled out of the truck's way, cursing him. 'Okay. See that open concrete area with all the people?'

'Yes,' I said, not asking which crowd he meant. The wide ribbon of concrete flowed west, like a second river, the buildings like a haphazard manmade cliff behind it.

'You got about ten minutes walk along that, then you get to the hospital. Can't get lost, just keep the river on your right, but keep your eyes open, it don't look like a hospital. Used to be some shopping mall.'

'Thanks, Jamil,' I said, dropping out of the truck with my pack falling out behind me. Jamil nodded, closed the door by remote and rumbled out of my life.

***

Nation of the Night

Dr Elke Bornstein, whom I was taken to speak to once I'd navigated through the haphazard maze of passages and rebuilt rooms, wasn't pleased when she heard I didn't have anywhere to stay after my surgery. They wouldn't let me stay in the hospital any longer than was absolutely necessary. 'That means, long enough to be sure the surgery didn't kill you,' she said. She was ash blonde, grey-eyed, and if she'd ever had a bedside manner, it had faded away long since amid the floating pack ice of her personality.

'How am I supposed to arrange accommodation?' I asked. 'I don't have money.'

Dr Bornstein stared at me as though I'd stopped speaking her language. I don't know why she was so incredulous. She knew where I was from, so surely an educated person like her knew the situation in my home. I tried to explain. 'Look, there's no infrastructure at all. Some of the phones work, because some people know how to set them up, but there's no—no businesses, no trade except barter. I got rides with truckers for free, just for helping them load and unload and keeping them awake at the wheel.'

Her expression didn't change. 'I can organise a bed for you in a men's hostel,' she said at last. 'It's attached to the hospital. You'll get a bed in a room crammed with men who have nowhere else to go. No one will do anything for you, but it will be clean and there's a bathroom with access to clean water. You can't go there yet, just after you have the surgery.'

'Thank you,' I said.

'Just one point. Don't tell them.'

'Tell them?'

'What your surgery was. Don't tell them you're FTM. Say it was heart surgery.'

'Okay.'

She nodded slightly, then waved a hand at me. 'Strip,' she ordered, with the same tone as she might have asked me to pass her an apple from the bowl on her table. This dispassion was all that helped me to do it. When I stood before her, she studied me.

'How old are you now?'

'Eighteen,' I said. Well, it could be true. Her look said she didn't believe it.

'You're lucky you're not large,' she said, gesturing at my chest. I avoided following her glance. Without the bindings, they felt pretty large to me. Ugly. 'I can use the peri-areolar method, which is less intrusive than some. Incision here and here to remove the tissue, lift the nipples, then your skin is pulled taut. Think of a drawstring bag.' I winced. 'If I think it's necessary, I'll have to put tubing in the incision, which will drain out under your armpits. A nurse will instruct you on how to empty the tubes of blood and other fluids. Do you have someone to help you?' I shook my head. 'You'll have to get some help.'

'How long will I be in the hospital?'

Dr Bornstein actually smiled. 'Only a few hours, before you go to the hostel. You're lucky that this isn't twenty years ago, or even ten. The pain medications these days are much more efficient than they used to be and of course we're able to give you the hormone implant rather than you needing to constantly take pills. You'll be out the same day and then you get two days in the hostel to be sure you're recovering.

Nation of the Night

After that, well, usually we recommend you come back for follow-up visits over the next few weeks, but you could have a problem with that. I'll write out some information for Cory Mitchell. He'll be able to remove the drains at least and monitor your recovery.'

'You're only talking about here.' I waved a hand at my chest, keeping my gaze on her. 'What about, you know, down here?'

'Cory only writes about a mastectomy,' she said, sounding no more than mildly interested. 'There was no mention of bottom surgery. You do know, don't you, that all this is a favour to him?'

I nodded, wondering just what favour Mitchell had done this particularly scary female. 'I know,' I said, wishing for a drink but not daring to ask even for a small amount of water.

'In any case, the recovery time necessary for that would be longer than you have available. The same goes for my theatre time. If another operation can be arranged, you will have to return here at some future date.'

She talked on, going into details of the surgery, which blurred in my memory quite fast. 'So that's what we'll do,' she said and I jumped a little; she'd never actually said we were in the psych test. 'You're adult and you are genuine. You need to be here in two days time for your surgery, first thing in the morning. The front desk will tell you whether it's going ahead then or if there's been a delay. They'll arrange your admission.'

'Will I see you?' I asked. I don't know why I said that, it was probably totally stupid.

Elke Bornstein's face relaxed fractionally. Her voice was a

49

little quieter, not quite so staccato, when she said, 'No. You won't see me. You'll be unconscious.'

I headed out of the hospital, whose name I still had not seen up anywhere, to survive two days as a stranger. Concrete spread out before me, all the way to the river. On the other bank, cliff-like buildings stared back. Other, newer-looking structures had been built wherever there was space, making a renovation nightmare of the northern bank. To either side, I could see small footbridges with people crossing them or fishing from them, though it was hard to believe fish could survive in the rubbish-strewn muddy water. There were scores of people camped outside the hospital on the concrete frontage and under the few trees; patients and visitors and street types as well. You couldn't always tell the difference, except the ones with the medical drips were most likely the patients. It looked like a random gathering, just people sitting on benches and curbs and up against walls, but I knew it was anything but. If I settled myself next to the wrong group, I could expect to get moved on and probably thumped a bit to encourage me to learn my place. Some of them watched me with an apathetic interest, others didn't even see me. It was, in a way, my first attempt to really pass, among people who didn't already know me, more of them than I had ever seen.

Some boys were gathered up against a metal fence to the left of the shopping mall/hospital's entrance. This encircled a rose garden, protecting it from the populace, off to one side, looking more pathetic than aesthetically pleasing. The

Nation of the Night

roses, not the boys. They were younger than me, I thought, mostly Caucasians, with a sprinkling of other races. Boy packs tend to separate according to such surface things. I walked over slowly, as though I wasn't even aware of what I was doing, and found a spot to sit nearby, my back against the fence. I was genuinely tired, the air of fatigue wasn't a lie, but I was much more aware of them than I tried to appear.

A couple of the boys approached, kicking empty cans aside just so I knew they were there. One prodded my sneaker. 'What do you think you're doing, man?' he asked.

I had to hide any sort of pleasure; the comment had been bluntly put and intended to irritate me.

I took my time about looking up. The two boys were around fourteen, better dressed than I was, in the sense that their clothes were not tied-together, aged hangovers from fourteen years ago, but their hair was lank and dirty, their faces scarred with acne. 'Parking my butt,' I replied after considering them. 'What does it look like?'

'This is our turf,' the spokesman said, giving my sneaker another meaningful prod. 'Like we say who can be here.'

'Yeah, well, I got to be somewhere for two days,' I said. 'Then I have to go back in there.' I pointed at the hospital.

'What's the matter with you?'

I was pretty sure Dr Bornstein's warning applied here as well. I decided to make the most of my paleness, due to avoiding all the hours of sunlight that I could. I was also thin for my height. 'Heart problem,' I said. 'What the fuck do you care?' I stared morosely at their feet, slumped as though my life was over right this moment.

Nightsiders   Sue Isle

'Then why are you out here?'

'I'm not admitted in the hospital until two days from now,' I said. 'I'm from Perth, I had a fucking long trip to get here and if you would get out of my face, I'd appreciate it!' I let my voice rise only slightly but was careful. Didn't want to screech like a girl.

'Come on,' the spokesman scoffed, but his tone was milder now. 'Nobody's allowed out of Perth now.'

'You got it the wrong way round,' I told him. 'Most everybody left when the Evac was declared.' There was little point in talking about loss of government and status quo and infrastructure with the street rats. I wouldn't have been able to even think about them myself if I hadn't been forced by my guardians to absorb schooling. I reminded myself, belatedly, to thank Daniel and Tom and Ellen Wakeling when I got home. 'Only a few people stayed. I was just a kid and I got separated from my folks. They don't worry about us coming over now because there's so few.'

'But this city don't let you stay,' the boy said. *Hm, not so ignorant as I'd thought.*

'Is it true there are vampires in Perth now?' the other boy asked, eager for new stories. He squatted, putting his face level with mine. His companion shot him a disapproving look and remained standing.

'What do you want?' I asked. 'To tell me I can't hang around or for me to tell you about Drainers?'

'So you're not staying?' the leader asked.

'I'm not staying. I get my op, I get better, I go home.' I pushed my legs out and prepared to stand. 'And I'll go find somewhere else to sit if that's what you guys really want.'

Nation of the Night

'You're in the shit if you stay here. We're okay now but later tonight, the cops come round and move everybody out. If you don't have anywhere to go, they'll dump you in the lockup and when they find out you're not local, they'll dump you in the desert.'

I slumped back and spread my hands. 'So, I got to find some guys who know this city and can maybe find me crash space?'

'What'd we do that for?'

'You want to know about the Nightside, I can tell you. You know some stories, I can tell you what it's really like.'

'Nightside?'

'We call Perth the Nightside mostly now, because we get around at night. It's too hot during the day in summer. Better in winter, I guess, but we're used to the dark. The bombing busted a lot of buildings as well as the underground railway, but we fixed some and we live in the tunnels. The city buildings are more like caves now, and you got to make sure the Drainers won't find you while you're asleep.'

Both of them were listening now.

'What's your name?' the leader asked.

'Ash.'

'I'm Brock. That's Jamie.'

'Hi.' I looked at each of them, then away. True wolf pack etiquette. Meet the eyes but don't stare. Acknowledge dominance, or, in this case, prior claim and local knowledge.

'Come on,' Brock said. 'We're going to head back anyway. You can tag along if you want, and you better know some good stuff.'

'No one else is going to know it,' I said and this seemed

53

Nightsiders
Sue Isle

to satisfy him. I followed them back to the heart of the pack and was introduced to about twenty boys at once. They asked my age and I said sixteen.

Maybe half the group dispersed when we left the hospital precincts, the ones who still had homes of a sort. The rest, the ones with no help, lived in a broken down, broken into terrace house in an area where no one went after dark unless he was stupid, I was assured. There was the trendy end of the CBD and then there was 'our end'. We ended up in a dusty room, eleven or twelve kids crowded around me.

'So is it true about the vampires?' Jamie asked.

'Kind of,' I conceded. 'I mean, they're people. They can come out in the day, like anyone else, only none of us do because it's so hot and you use too much water if you move around much. But we live in the night because it's more comfortable. They use it to hide. If somebody is off on his own, sometimes the Drainers will grab him and take him off somewhere no one will hear the screaming.' There was a brief murmur of appreciation; this was the kind of story they liked. 'They might only strip him of everything he's got, clothes, supplies, any water, but if they're really hungry or thirsty, they might tap his blood, or outright kill him. They don't do that a lot, because when they kill someone, we get stirred up and we go after them, into their hiding places.'

'You ever do that?' Jamie again.

'A couple of times,' I admitted. 'There was a girl who went missing. She lived in the same building as me and one night her friends set up this huge screaming and crying that she'd been dragged off, into the underground tunnel beneath the city where the trains used to run. So some of us went

Nation of the Night

with them into the tunnel to try and find her. It was so dark you couldn't see this,' and I waved a hand in front of my face. 'We didn't have any batteries, so we had to use fire torches and they only make this little circle of light around you. We went in there in a pack, tight together, because the Drainers might grab one of us off the fringes. They didn't have anything to lose then. We could hear folk, far off, whispering and scuttling like rats.'

'Did you get her back?' A girl this time. She was even younger than Jamie and had a faint but clear voice. She was plainly imagining herself in the role of the kidnapped girl.

I thought about making up an exciting ending for my tale, but in the end shook my head. I'd only mess it up. 'No. We didn't find her. We almost got lost ourselves, but we got out. At least there were no more stealings, so we scared them that much.'

'Did anyone tell the police?' Brock asked, disapproving of us, or our failure, it was hard to tell.

'They wouldn't have gone in. There are only a few of them, they're kind of an outpost to keep sending reports back E… I mean, here. If they'd gone in, probably the same would have happened to them.'

'How could you get lost, if it was a train tunnel?' Brock had certainly paid attention.

'Because it's all broken up. When the city got bombed, back before the Evac, they hit the train tunnels dead on and there are big craters and caves now, off to the side. So you could wander for a while before you found out you were in a dead end. The Drainers dig too, they've made tunnels just wide enough for people to move in, so they can get around

Nightsiders   Sue Isle

the crater sites without coming out into the sun. But they're tough, they can move in the daylight without any trouble. Daniel says they're a mutation. He's a professor, he knows about stuff like that,' I added with as much authority as I could. I didn't want to get bogged down about scientific detail I couldn't explain.

'That's shit,' Jamie decreed, evidently disappointed by my showing against 'the vampires'. 'Perth never got bombed by anyone. I went to school and they never told us about anything like that.'

'They tell you people don't live in Perth any more too, don't they?' I challenged him. 'It happened. It was before I was born but you can see where all the damage happened. The Indonesians hit the desal plants and—and other important places. The city tried to recover but it was too expensive to fix it all, so all that helped lead to the Evac.' I looked at Jamie but either he was out of arguments or busy thinking of new ones. I'd realised, to my surprise, that he and the others couldn't actually see me that well. The dark, to them, was a handicap, streetwise as they were.

'So tell me about this city,' I said, seizing my temporary advantage. 'Why's it so packed with people around here?'

They looked at me as though I'd taken stupid pills.

'Almost nobody got cars,' Brock said. 'So everybody lives close as they can, you know. If you've got money, you get to live in those places next to the river. Politicians and people like that. They've got nightclubs and pubs and everything in there but the guards don't let you in if you don't live there. We're undesirable elements. That's what the old folks say.'

56

Nation of the Night

He was all of fourteen and he sounded like an old granddad himself. What he said didn't sound like the historical Melbourne I'd heard about. What I knew was from people who had been there more than two decades before. Those sources told me that it was a big city, containing some five million people at its peak, and that the inner city never shut down, blazing lights and music and entertainment all night and selling everything you could wish to buy. That this didn't happen now wasn't a surprise; not to me, but the dismissive tone in Brock's voice about 'the old folks' did surprise me. You're not at home, I reminded myself, noting the murmur of agreement go around the kids sitting in the dark, dusty room. 'What old folks?' I asked all the same. 'Your folks?'

'Nah, not them. You know. The ones in charge, the ones who try and tell us what to do,' said Jamie. Someone coughed and spat, but I couldn't tell if it was in response or not. There was a rattle outside, which made me think of sticks falling on a roof, then a slamming sound. Brock jumped up, swearing instinctively, 'Fuck!'

Just then another of the pack slammed into the room, not trying to be quiet. 'Raid!' he said.

'Just go,' Brock said to me, getting up quickly. 'Come back here in a few hours, they'll be gone then.'

Good advice, except for one thing. As everybody scattered, it was impossible for me to make any speed towards any exit, given that I didn't know them. A bottleneck of kids blocked my way to the front door and when I did get to it, it was only to be confronted by a floodlight torch and

57

Nightsiders

Sue Isle

a phalanx of police. Yelling beyond them told me some of the kids had been grabbed or at least blocked off. Someone gunned an engine. Beyond the floods, the street was dark, not that I could see anything much at all. I squeezed my eyes shut and held my hand in front of them for good measure.

'What's your name?' a cop asked me.

'Ash.'

'Ash what? Don't waste my time. I've had a gutful of you kids breaking into places. Your full name, smart arse.'

'Ash Henderson.'

'You're not on the list.' He tapped the electronic pad he held, glanced at his partner, who shrugged. The cops behind them split off to go after another couple of kids. 'Doesn't matter. Come on, you're going for a ride.'

So I spent a night in a cell, instead of a broken down house which had hardly needed any breaking to enter. It wasn't too comfortable but it was dry and warm enough. They wanted me to take a shower but I didn't think there'd be any privacy, so I refused. One of the cops swore at me but they didn't forcibly strip me, which I'd been scared they'd do. In the end they shoved me into a holding cell that already had five guys in it and I spent the night awake, especially alert after one of them hit on me in no uncertain terms.

'Go to one of the work centres or leave the city,' a watch-house officer told me in the morning.

'What's a work centre?' I asked one of my companions of the night, who stumbled past me, scratching and spitting. It sounded like a place you went to find jobs, but why would a cop say that to a kid he thought was a vagrant?

58

Nation of the Night

The guy laughed, which created a horrible coughing/bubbling sound in his lungs. 'Somewhere they make you work, man. They give you some little fucking cot to sleep on and crap food, but they'll wake you at dawn and you move rubbish or dead trees or shit like that.'

This had the note of personal experience. I dredged up what little I knew about the welfare traditions of civilised cities. 'Do they give you an allowance—money—so you can buy food or whatever?'

He spat a huge gob of phlegm on to the footpath, narrowly missing my feet, which were bare. My shoes had been torn loose somewhere during the crowded ride to the lockup, or perhaps later inside, I couldn't remember. A light rain was falling and I had to jerk my attention away from it to hear his reply.

'Where the fuck have you been, under a fucking rock?'

'Just about,' I said but he wasn't listening. He staggered off down the road, his goal to get away from the watch-house, that much was clear. I walked the other way, through the car park, which I thought would take me in the rough direction of the river and the hospital. It might be worth trying that hostel. Just for one night before the op. They might let me stay if I did some work for them or something.

My chest was aching and uncomfortable, which meant the bindings under my loose shirt had probably slipped. I usually took them off when I slept, if I was in a safe place. The drunk tank hadn't rated. I tried to cheer myself up imagining my future a few days away. I wouldn't care how much my chest, or anywhere else, hurt then.

Nightsiders Sue Isle

I did find a public toilet with at least one undamaged booth door that I could shut while I took my shirt off and did my best to restore the bindings. I rubbed my chest hard on the red lines gouged into my flesh, angrily controlling an urge to cry when I saw myself bare. I pulled the bindings closed and clipped them together. Flat once more, I flushed the toilet and emerged, washing in the basin until I figured I could walk around without getting arrested again, at least while daylight lasted.

Now for that hostel. I needed some answers.

'No,' said the big Maori-looking guy who blocked the doorway of a low, grey stone building a few minutes walk from the hospital. It was much newer and much less well-constructed. 'If you're not an admitted patient, you can't stay here. After you get your surgery, you're allowed a maximum of three nights.'

'But I got chucked into prison because the police found me in a squatter house.'

He began to slide the door closed, but I kept my foot in the way. 'I can work, some cleaning or cooking or whatever, help any kids with their reading...'

He stopped sliding the door shut. I had already braced my foot for some pain to add to the bruises from hard pavements and a still-bleeding cut from a shattered bottle. 'You're a teacher?' He looked extremely dubious and I reminded myself that he probably guessed me at a few years younger than my age. Also barefoot and unkempt.

'No,' I said quickly before he decided I was bullshitting. 'But my guardian is a teacher and sometimes I help in the school.' No need for too much precision here, though it was

Nation of the Night

actually true that some of my community work was helping out old lady Wakey.

The guy thought some more. 'Okay,' he said finally. 'I know some people—not living here—who've got kids. Even a few days; they could use somebody to help the kids with reading and numbers.'

'I can help after I get out of hospital,' I said. 'Even if I can't move around, I can do that.'

He laughed. 'You're going to be hurting too damn much to help anyone for some time, kid. Nobody gets to stay here unless they've had major work done! Okay, you've got a deal. You go help these people today, tonight you get a cot, then after your op, when you're up and about, you give us a week of teaching time before you head off? Or else if you decide to stay, we can work out something else.'

'Deal,' I said, too dizzy with dehydration and discomfort to think any further. I only hoped these people he was talking about didn't live way across the city.

The unit he took me to was only a few streets away, still in the CBD. It was a cramped little flat, sandwiched on the fifth level of a bulky grey tower, bare of plants and colours but full of rubbish lying on the walkways and stairs. People, mostly adolescent males, stood around and watched us with empty, predatory eyes.

'This is my sister lives here,' the orderly, who had belatedly introduced himself as Mike, told me, a hint of threat in his voice. 'Her man was local but he took off. Her and me come from New Zealand, so her kids don't get school access. You behave yourself and don't give her any crap, hear me?'

'How stupid do I look?' I demanded, instead of saying

61

Nightsiders   Sue Isle

something conciliatory, but I was sick of that. Fortunately,
Mike thought that was funny and slapped me so hard on
the back that I nearly fell forward on to the concrete steps
we were climbing.

'Not that dumb, I guess,' he said. 'I got to look out for
her, that's all. I'll explain to Nella, then you stay here a few
hours and I'll come get you when I get off work, drop you
back to the hostel. I sleep over, keep an eye on things, break
any heads that need it.'

Mike's sister Nella kept a wary stare fixed on me while her
brother explained. Behind her in the flat, I could hear kids
shrieking, so there were at least two.

'I dunno, Mike,' she said when he got to the end.

'Come on, the kids could do with some reading lessons,
right?'

'I guess.' She was a tall broad woman, very much the
female equivalent of Mike. I had no doubt she could take
care of me, were I to lose my mind and try to attack her, and
I saw her realise the same thing as she evaluated me. 'Okay,
but make sure you're here by six.' Mike promised and headed
off and she told me to come in.

The interior was a smallish room, with a three-seater
couch, two chairs and a low table, all done in muted browns
and creams. Through a door at the back I could see a kitchen
and another door opened to what I supposed was a bedroom.
On the couch, bedding had been folded over the back to
get it out of the way during the day. Two kids, maybe ten
and eight, were screaming and rolling around on the floor
between the couch and one of the chairs, where a third one,
even smaller, perched and squawked.

62

Nation of the Night

'Want a glass of water?' Nella asked me.

'Yes. Thank you,' I said, surprised. Offering water was a particularly hospitable act, at least it was at home. She went into the kitchen and ran water in the sink, I could see it splashing out of the tap and watched, mesmerised, as she took an upended glass and filled it. When she gave it to me, I drank slowly—gulping was always rude—and nodded; it was very clean water.

'I'll introduce you to the kids,' Nella said, 'then I got to go out and do some stuff. Are you okay with minding them?'

'What don't you want them doing?' I asked. I meant it as a simple statement of fact; what are the parameters, but she laughed.

'You say that like you can make it happen. They've got to stay in the flat and not wreck things, anything else is up to you.'

Did she just want a babysitter for a few hours? I wondered. I couldn't see any reading matter. There was a television but it looked rather battered and perhaps didn't work, otherwise Nella would surely have had it doing babysitting duty already. I would've been tempted. I'd seen television, or at least DVDs, when the generators were working, which wasn't often.

'Look—your brother said something about them not being able to go to school. What does that mean? Have they been to school at all?'

'Oh, sure. Rafael had the most,' she said, pointing to one of the scrappers. 'He's ten, so he had almost four years in New Zealand before we came here. Emiri's eight, she's had two and Sam's too young.'

63

'I don't get it,' I said bluntly. 'Why can't they go to school? Why did you come here if it meant they couldn't go to school?'

She still smiled a little, but not as though she thought I was funny. 'Don't know much, do you?'

I wanted to object, but she hadn't said it as though she was trying to offend me. 'I'm not from here, as you know. I thought this city was supposed to be still going, you know, civilisation working, the lights on and all that.'

Nella shrugged as though all that was nothing to her. 'Well—it keeps going by tightening the purse strings, you know. Immigrants don't have the same rights as locals, so when the schools are full, that's it. They let us come because they need people for the grunt jobs, but they don't spend money on us to let our kids go to their schools. We got a little community school they'll go to when Mike and I make a bit more money, but like he says, right now they're stuck.' She headed into the bedroom and came back with a couple of stiff-backed, brightly coloured books. 'They can read off these, we brought them along with us.'

'No problem.'

'Well, good luck.' She had to walk over to the two oldest and pull them apart so she could introduce them to me and tell them I'd be 'minding' them while she had to go out. They immediately screamed and begged to come along, they were bored, they didn't want to stay in here, they didn't want to *read*! I didn't blame them. I'd have been climbing the walls in much the same way.

'See you in a couple of hours,' Nella said hastily, grabbed a couple of hessian bags and was gone, followed by the yells

Nation of the Night

of the three kids. I went over to a chair with the books, sat down and began to look through them, giving the ferals a chance to get used to the idea of being shut in the flat with a stranger.

Finally they turned around from the front door to look at me. Rafael and Emiri did, anyway. Sam was still in his chair, making that weird squawking noise but not actually looking at anyone. 'Hi,' I said. 'My name's Ash.'

'Are you a teacher?' Emiri asked suspiciously.

'No. I'm going to be staying at the hostel where Mike works. I help out in the school they have at home so he asked if I could give you guys a reading lesson.' I looked down at the book in my hands. A Doctor Seuss. 'If you don't want a reading lesson, that's up to you.' I turned a page as though I planned to read the book to myself and ignore them. Dr Seuss is an artistic genius, or so Tom Roper had told me.

Rafael plopped himself down on the couch and after a moment, his sister joined him. They looked much alike, broad-featured, black-haired kids, wearing shorts and t-shirts of garish colours. 'I can already read,' Rafael claimed. 'Better than her.'

Predictably, Emiri began to yell and punched him in the shoulder. I turned in the chair and ignored them. My gaze fell on Sam, who didn't appear to have noticed the commotion.

'Hey,' I said, when there was a break in the noise, 'can either of you tell me what's up with Sam? Is he deaf?'

'No, he's hortistic,' Emiri said. 'You won't be able to teach him how to read.'

'I'm not doing so great with you guys either,' I said and held out the book. 'Somebody. Read aloud so I can hear how

65

Nightsiders   Sue Isle

good or crappy you are.' That made them giggle, but Rafael grabbed the book and took up the challenge. I stopped him after a few verses and got Emiri to try. Two years at school isn't anything like enough, but she was almost as good as her older brother. I decided we were doing okay.

I did try to get Sam's attention to *The Cat*, sitting on his chair with him and holding the book in front of him, but true to Emiri's word, he didn't engage. He got off the chair and went over to the one I'd vacated, picking at the material of the back and generally behaving as though he was alone in the room. I'd seen kids like that at home and while I didn't know much about teaching autistics, I knew they needed a lot more one-on-one than normal kids, because they essentially didn't speak our language.

'You better not bother Sam or he'll start screaming and you won't be able to stop him,' Emiri predicted.

'Okay,' I said. I looked around the flat again, though I'd pretty well seen everything my eyes could rest on in the first few minutes. Even without the bedding on the couch and the suitcases, which seemed to double as clothing drawers, lying against the sitting room wall, plus a variety of plastic junk, this place was cramped. For one person it would be cramped. For five—assuming Mike stayed here when he wasn't on duty or doing sleepovers at the hostel—it must be a complete crush.

That was a long, long day and I owed Miss Wakeling—I wasn't going to call her Wakey Wakey any more—a lifetime's worth of gratitude for all the stuff she'd taught me that I never knew I'd learned.

Nation of the Night

That night, Mike came and got me and took me back to the hostel. He also, to my intense gratitude, brought me a pair of scuffed but intact rubber boots, which made the journey much more comfortable. More so than the men's hostel, where as many bunks were crammed as could fit into each room. The dormitory room was already darkened for sleep and all the beds but one occupied by people breathing with various degrees of difficulty and pain. 'Act sick,' he murmured as he left me by the empty cot. I was so tired by then that it wasn't hard, I just took off the boots and lay down, fully dressed. No way was I taking anything else off here.

Next day, Mike directed me over to Admissions, a food hall area still doing some business. Once I was there, I settled down to wait, which proved to be for most of the day, until a couple of guys with a wheelchair came and got me to take me to theatre.

I woke, with no memory of dreaming. I was in a wide corridor with other wheeled beds, containing patients, against the walls. Time jumped again, though I didn't remember sleeping, but Mike was suddenly there by the bed. He was soaked, including his clothes and his hair.

'How did you get wet?' I asked.

Not only did Mike stare at me, but also a couple of patients, one on crutches, one with his head swathed in bandages as though he planned to audition for some movie featuring tomb robbers and Egyptian mummies. 'Not from around here, are ya?' the guy on crutches asked.

Mike was laughing, theatrically wiping tears from his eyes. 'Fuck me,' he muttered. 'Didn't you see the storm?'

'What storm?'

'Never mind. I'll show you later. Come on, I got to take you along to the hostel. When we get there you can sleep. You get forty-eight hours and then you're out, no extensions allowed. Sorry, but there's been some emergencies come in, broken limbs and that from storm damage.'

I started to get out of the gurney.

The next thing I knew, I was being wheeled along a different corridor. Mike's voice rumbled behind me. 'You back with us? Don't get up, okay? I'll only have to pick you up again. You're full of pain meds, so it won't hurt for awhile but the doc says you won't remember how to move for awhile.'

When we reached the hostel, he did pick me up, but only to deposit me in a narrow bed. 'When you have to move, do it slowly,' was his last bit of advice.

I followed Mike's advice for the next two days. The pain medication wore off. I didn't get any more injections but they gave me some pills with instructions to ration them, because I wasn't getting any more of those either. All around me were men recovering from surgeries, or not, too absorbed in their own worlds of pain to care about anyone else. A nurse came by once to help me with the draining of fluid from the surgical wounds—she said Dr Bornstein sent her—but apart from that, no one spoke to me.

On the third day, Mike came back for me and said we were going to Nella's place.

Nation of the Night

The world wasn't just wet, when I got out into it. It was cold. I thought I knew cold; it was that windy winter time when you got out your jacket, the time when you felt invigorated, wanting to move and try new things. We always did our best thinking for new performances in the winters. Daniel had more students then. But this cold bit right into my bones and into my fresh scars. I felt the chill deep in my chest, even though Mike had brought me a coat to wear, 'out of the lost and found,' he said. It looked and smelled as though it had recently been skinned off the body of a camel, but I hugged it desperately close as I followed Mike. I could walk but my energy seemed to have dribbled through my feet and out. I was very grateful for those rubber boots he'd given me.

'Don't die on me, will you?' Mike grumbled, but his look was more concerned than his words. 'You want to go back? I can call one of the docs to look at you.'

'No, I'm okay!' I had to shout over the sudden stronger gusting of the icy wind. 'Not used to this cold. It's unbelievable—in summer.'

'Yeah, well, people say it used to get hot and dry in summer but not these days,' Mike agreed. 'Nearly there.'

This road slanted downhill to Nella's street, where we splashed through an unofficial creek. I saw Mike look at the water, then track across to the units. He looked worried but he didn't say anything to me as we climbed the stairs. Nella opened her door only as far as she had to and we squeezed in.

'Bet you're glad you're not on the bottom floor now,' her brother greeted her, grinning.

Nightsiders   Sue Isle

'Yeah, but not too much better if we get cut off again,' Nella retorted. 'Or if bits of the building fall off!'

Her kids were screaming and fighting again. When they saw Mike, they raced over to attack him instead of each other, except for Sam, who was in his world and didn't notice us.

I sat down, trying not to gasp for air the way I wanted to do. A brisk hike and five flights of stairs weren't on the doctor's recommendations for recovery. Nella's attention went immediately to me.

'He's okay, Nell,' Mike assured her. 'But he had surgery two days ago. They move 'em on from the hostel quick as they can, you know that, so when I said he had somewhere to go—he can stay here, right?'

'I'll be heading home soon,' I said, right as Nella said,

'I guess so, but we're going to need more supplies, Mike.'

Nella wasn't unsympathetic, I knew that, but I also knew from my own life that when supplies were short, the stranger was not welcome. You only had time and energy to spare for your own kin, anyone not of your tribe was excess. I was relieved to feel the tightness of my chest begin to ease, now that I was out of the chill and no longer moving.

'You can't head home while this is going on,' Mike told me, raising his voice easily above the screeching of Emiri and Rafael. 'You have to catch a ride with a truckie, right? No way they'll even get out of their depot. Even those big rigs stay home. You listen to your Uncle Mike.'

I walked to the front and held the curtain aside so that I could look at the rain. It was sheeting so hard that I couldn't really see anything else. Nothing alive was out there, it would

Nation of the Night

have been knocked down and swept away. The noise was incredible; something like the windstorms we got at home but harsher, as though the rain was spears that could beat through brick and tile and destroy us. My chest hurt, but who cared? I was free now.

'Hey,' Mike called, 'don't get the idea you can go play in that, okay? Bigger people than you get killed in storms like that.'

The kids thought that was hilarious; Uncle Mike telling another adult the sort of thing they probably heard all the time. 'Can you tell us about where you come from?' Emiri asked when the laughter finally faded. Those kids could drown out the rain when they tried.

Not only the kids, but Nella and Mike, settled down to listen to me try to explain what it was like to live in a mostly empty city of heat and wind, where 'winter' meant only a cooling, never freezing, and where our tribes were constantly at work repairing the places we lived in.

'The vegetables have to be sheltered,' I said, 'so that's why they use buildings without roofs, so they can get some sun, but it's easy to put shadenets over the top. Most of us take turns there. There's one particular mob mostly looks after the food and trades for other stuff. And there are some fish in the river but you got to be careful, because you can get sick if you eat the wrong fish.'

'How do you know if they're the wrong fish?' Rafael asked.

'Sometimes you can tell, other times you got to eat a bit and wait to see if you feel all right, then you keep eating. Some folk get so hungry they just scoff it down and then,

71

Nightsiders   Sue Isle

well, bad things can happen.' I was cautious about being too graphic about food poisoning deaths in front of protected kids like these.

'Do they bloat up and turn funny colours and die?' Emiri asked.

'Uh, yeah, pretty much.'

'But you got crazies, don't you?' Nella asked, sounding just like her daughter. 'We heard from some of the last ones they let come here, that there were some yobs just smashing things and—and hurting folks.'

'We got crazies. Some people think we're all crazy in different ways,' I said slowly. I was not going to talk about the Drainers and their ways to this audience. A mob of teenaged streetkids was one thing. 'I don't think we'd suit this city now.'

'Maybe that's why they don't let any more in,' suggested Mike. 'Did you know that? If you didn't go home and they caught you, they'd just put you outside.'

'The doctor said I should stay,' I objected.

'Vanish, yeah, a lot do. But if they found you, you'd find yourself in the desert and no choice but to keep going thataway.' His thumb indicated the distant Nightside to the west. 'You got some time, don't get me wrong. I think it's two weeks you can stay, I'd need to check.'

'It's not like this side of the desert is so great either,' Nella grumbled. 'Not letting the kids go to school, for one.'

'What's with that?' I asked curiously. 'You guys are residents, right?'

'So long as we've got jobs—or one of us has got a job,' she added with a glance at her brother.

72

Nation of the Night

'So, uh, why didn't you stay in New Zealand?'

'Even worse there,' Mike said. 'The 'flu got NZ pretty bad, worse than Australia. The schools were like just disease farms, a lot of kids and teachers died. Nobody likes to be part of any sort of big group now.' He shrugged, not able to fully explain but I thought I had the picture. Long term trauma was something anyone in the Nightside understood.

'How long were you at school?' Nella asked me.

'Uh—eight years, nine. I think I was five when I started and fourteen when I stopped doing regular school, but a year or so back, I moved in with the professor I told you about, and you can't avoid getting taught around Daniel. So I'm okay with maths and he taught me some history and other stuff.'

'How old are you now?' Mike asked.

'Eighteen, maybe nineteen.'

'Christ. You look about fifteen.'

'Malnutrition,' I said, which was half-true. They seemed to accept it. 'I got left as a kid. My mother abandoned me to come East and it was a while before somebody found me. I don't remember it that well.'

'You ever see her again?' Mike asked.

'No.' Truth was, she had never been more than a shadow to me, a dim recollection of tallness, and a hand holding mine painfully hard, dragging me … then letting go and moving quickly away. I could even have imagined that. Daniel had said there was no way to be sure and in any case, there was no point in dwelling on things. I didn't even know whether my father had been around then. I had no images of him at all.

Nightsiders   Sue Isle

'Tell me about the school,' Nella said. 'What do they teach the little kids? How many students are there?'

So I spent the rest of the evening trying to drag up every scrap I possibly could about Ellen Wakeling and my first years under her command, as well as the other teachers who had come and gone during that time, and about the students, Ali and Minh and Yarran and the rest. The rain eased a little and Mike went out for supplies, but Nella continued to listen as eagerly, or more so, than her children. At last I had to beg a halt to rest, because my head was aching and I felt dizzy with fatigue.

Not even the kids' noise kept me awake. I slept in the bed she made for me on the couch.

Mike didn't return until much later. All I knew was that he was there in the morning, tired and shaken and with bruises on his face from encountering a gang of looters around the supply stores, wherever they were. I woke to find Nella bandaging his arm, which was streaming blood. She was fretting about whether he'd be able to work.

'Nell, work's about the best bloody place I could be. It's a hospital! They'll take a look and make sure my arm's not going to drop off.'

'That knife was probably filthy,' she snapped.

'I had my tetanus shot…'

'Some of those bugs can beat the shots.'

'So I ought to get there soon as I can. Listen, you'll be fine. You've got plenty of food now and the kid will be here to help you out.'

'He's just up from major surgery. What can he do?'

'Keep the kids from driving you crazy, for one.' Mike

Nation of the Night

wasn't snapping back at her. He knew as well as she did what this could mean and how anxious she was. 'Come on, it'll be okay. Pretty soon we'll have enough put by for Rafe and Em to go to the community school and maybe even for Sam to go to crèche, that'll give you a real break. Then you'll be able to work like you want.'

'There's somebody's roof in the street below,' she said. Her mind was wandering. She went on, more coherently. 'That damn wind, it blew the rain like it was steel sheeting, knocked the roof clean off and nobody's come to help those folks yet. I don't think it'll ever be safe for the kids to go out and play, Mike. It's been three months. We ought to go home.'

'We can't,' he said gently. 'It's as crazy there as here and even wetter.'

'We could go with him, you know.'

Mike was silent. I'd woken on my side, facing away from them, so it was easy enough to pretend I was asleep. I didn't like to eavesdrop, not when I hardly knew them, but this was too good.

'To the Nightside?' he asked. 'You heard what Ash said about it. The heat in the summer—and they get wind-storms too, in the winter. They have to keep building and rebuilding.'

'They help each other,' she said. 'There's so few of them that they're like a tribe, the way our people were once. There's Aboriginal tribes too. I think he said they run the lands outside the city, but inside the city is the white folks' tribe. And they've got a school. They care about the kids, Mike, any kids, no matter where they come from.'

75

'That's crazy,' he said but from the way he spoke, I knew she'd got to him, at least partly. 'Nobody goes the other way.'

'They do,' I said, deciding to betray myself. I rolled over, with care, and realised I was going to have to ask Mike for some help and of necessity come clean to him, or else go in to the hospital. 'The truckies, remember, and the camel trains. And always some people who've been wandering, on the road so long they don't remember for sure where they started out. Even some who came here and decided they didn't like it.'

'You know anyone?' Mike challenged me. 'I mean, anyone who came back to live?'

'Not immediate friends,' I had to admit, 'but I know who some of them are. I know people who know returners.'

Mike sighed. 'Well, right now I got to return to work. You okay or do you need to come in?'

'I think I should come with you. Just to get checked out,' I added, seeing Nella's sudden look of dismay at the imminent loss of her babysitter and crowd calmer. 'I can come right back here on my own.'

'Suit yourself,' Mike said dubiously. 'There's usually a hell of a long wait to see anyone.'

'I just need to see a nurse. I need help with, you know.' I waved vaguely at my bandages.

'That should be all right,' Mike conceded. 'Come on then.'

I followed him back through the flooded streets, unable to keep my gaze from the children playing in the water. It would have been so cool to be able to join them.

Nation of the Night

At the hospital, he found me an enrolled nurse who helped me drain fluid from the tubes, checked the general state of my recovery and cleaned me up before putting on fresh bandages. She told me I should be fine to go home, with the clear implication that I shouldn't darken the hospital doors again. I wanted to talk to Elke Borenstein but after Mike's warning about the waiting time, decided not to ask. Mike was gone about his duties, so I made my way slowly back to the flat. I felt more able, I decided, and looked at the dirty water swirling around the pavements. As soon as it receded, I'd visit whatever truck depots I could find and see whether anyone was heading west and could use a passenger to help him or her stay awake.

That night Mike and Nella had another argument about conditions in this city and the merits of travelling west.

'Anybody would think you guys were married,' I said when Mike clumped into the living room, where I was again playing storyteller/minder to Emiri and Rafe. Sam was in his room, doing who knew what, but at least it was quiet.

'You can't divorce sisters,' Mike grumped. It hadn't seemed to occur to him that he could just walk off from Nella and the whole chaotic kid tribe. Maybe that was what family meant.

'You know, you can't come with me right now anyway,' I said, deciding I had to make that clear. 'If all five of you want to come, you got to set something up with a camel caravan, and it'll be a tough trip, believe me. The caravan owners will skin you for everything you've got and we can't do too much for you, at the other end. I can set up crash space but that's

Nightsiders   Sue Isle

just what it'll be. You'll have to reclaim your own house or there's people you can pay to do it for you. If you can pay.'

'I get the picture,' Mike sighed.

'It's not … organised,' I said, wishing I could show him the buildings broken by bombings or just time, few of them safe enough for people to live in. My building was five storeys high and it was one of those few, but we worked on it constantly and even so, there were happenings. A step falling out beneath someone's feet, causing a fall and a broken leg. Part of a ceiling falling in and killing the people sleeping below. 'You get in trouble, your friends help if they can but that's all. If there's a fire, you got to put it out yourselves. You're always scrounging for food and good water.'

'You want to go home to that,' Nella said quickly, from the doorway to the kitchen. 'Why?'

'They're my family.'

'And they would help, wouldn't they, if you got in trouble?'

'Same as I'd help them.'

'That's what we don't have here,' she said, looking at her brother.

'We don't because we don't come from here,' he said. 'The locals got family and they got hospitals which may be as overcrowded as a bloody rat's nest, but they still got them.'

Nella called Rafe and Emiri to settle down to bed and for Mike and I to be quiet. We did, while she wrangled Sam into the quietest corner in the furthest room.

'We better get some rest too,' Mike said.

My chest still hurt but it was manageable. I wouldn't need any more help to drain fluid and I had the implant to take

Nation of the Night

care of medications for a year. Beyond that, I would either have to establish a source of T-pills or return for another implant, but that could be settled later. Right now, I had what I needed to go home and I needed to go, rain or not, before I became a drain on Mike and Nella or worse, before Nella decided a city with no rain was her earthly paradise.

Mike slept in the lounge area too, on the floor. All three kids were in the other room with their mother, which probably didn't give Nella anything like a good night's rest. I was hoping she and Mike would at least snooze, because the moment they did, I was going to be out the front door.

Finally there was quiet. Sam had been making a monotonous growling sort of noise, for reasons unknown, but that had stopped at last. I lay still, listening to Mike breathing and trying to make out any sound of restlessness from the others. It sounded calm. I got off the couch, still dressed except for the camel coat, which I had thrown over the back. It had a pocket that would zip, where I had stowed the rest of the painkilling meds Dr Borenstein had given me. These were the only things, aside from my changed body, that I would be taking out of Melbourne with me.

I opened the front door as quietly as I could, not even realising I was holding my breath until I had to take a gasp of air. It clicked shut behind me and I hurried down the stairs until my chest hurt and then I slowed. There was no betrayed yell from behind me or slap of feet on concrete.

Even so, I felt like I had betrayed them. Nella needed my help with the kids and I owed her for the food I'd eaten and shelter I'd used.

Nightsiders   Sue Isle

I headed north, to the inner city depot Mike had identified for me, showing me on a mud map he drew. The area was called Flagstaff Gardens, but he'd assured me there weren't any gardens now, just industrial premises. Within moments I was soaked by a light and windy rain, up to my knees in water. I tried to ignore it and just go, the way I ignored heat and sweat and thirst back home, but cold and wind were different. It felt like being stabbed. Even the street gangs weren't around, probably holed up in their odorous lairs. I thought of the kids who slunk like rats through derelict buildings and hoped they were all right. They were the ones who might do okay back in my world.

At home, no one got to sneak up on me. Everyone who survived was good at taking care of themselves that way. But in the windy and soaked surrounds of this occupied city, all the sounds were strange to me and I'd spent so much time scared and isolated that nothing stood out.

That's my only possible excuse for not noticing anything wrong before something struck me on the head.

I woke up as one uninterrupted throb of pain, in a dark, musty-smelling house, with a vaguely familiar group of younger teenagers around me. A moment later, I realised they had also tied me up. A boy, also familiar, crouched in front of me.

'You're taking us back with you,' he said. My brain struggled for his name. Fourteen or so, I thought, stripy … American creature, no, English … badger…

'Brock,' I said.

Nation of the Night

'Winner.' He didn't smile or look like a kid. Somebody stuck something sharp into my arm and I yelled, whipping it away. 'We know about you. We asked at the hospital.'

'Yeah, right, like the hospital is going to tell strange kids all about somebody.'

'You keep asking,' said a girl. I had to twist to the side to see her. She'd been there too in the dark house, the night of the raid. Her name was maybe Gertie, no, Greta. 'You find somebody not too high up, who does stuff, who maybe wants something, they'll tell you.'

'You got to get us to the Nightside, make 'em let us in,' Brock said.

'There's no—nothing to be let into,' I said, trying to get up off the carpet, but they'd tied my wrists and ankles too tightly and all I did was flop around. 'I told you!'

'Nobody telling you what to do,' Brock said. 'You make your own place and if you're tough, nobody takes it or chases you out of it. You get to sleep in the day and go wild at night.' His eyes gleamed and I realised how these kids had taken my stories, how my words had meant totally different things to them than they did to me.

'You get thirsty,' I said, hard and fast, trying to boil it down so they'd see it in one piece. 'Your water runs out and you have to wait to dark to get to the river for some more. Then you have to boil it and put stuff in it so it doesn't burn through your gut and make you throw up all night. And you still haven't got anything to eat. You go to the farms but they don't need any workers there and they've got big guys at the gates who hurt you if you try to get in. Maybe you get sick

81

Nightsiders   Sue Isle

and there's no medicine, no doctor, except some guy who was apprenticed to a real doctor, who keeps saying he can't do this or this because he doesn't have the drugs.'

'Hey,' said Brock, 'doesn't sound too fucking different from here.'

I was sick of this. I hurt and I almost felt sorry for them too, but they'd tied me up and hit me. I could have a concussion but if I did, I was going to have to work through it on my own. 'Let me loose then. It's not like I can run from the lot of you.'

Brock started to say something and I believe he would have cut the bonds or told the girl to let me go, when a great thumping and yelling started at the front door. A deep yelling—a man. Some of the kids piled up around the front door to try to stop the guy coming in, but the flimsy door burst open and I saw a broad-shouldered shape I suddenly realised was Mike. From my position tied up on the floor, I couldn't see whether any of the kids had weapons, but knives was a reasonable bet.

'Mike, they're armed,' I yelled for good measure. That was all I got out before the girl, Greta, who was maybe twelve, thumped me in my sore ribs so hard that I couldn't breathe out. I just froze, trying to cheat the pain. By then Mike was in the room, pushing the boys aside as though they were his little niece and nephews. I felt something drop to the floor and hit my face; the cold metal of a knife.

'Ash,' Mike said, 'I could use some help—oh.' He shoved Brock and knelt to grab the knife, quickly slitting the bonds on my wrists. I sat up, ignoring the discomfort of my stomach muscles, and began to work at my ankle bonds myself. Mike

82

Nation of the Night

was busy fending off Brock and Jamie, swearing at them with enthusiasm. I saw him shove Jamie against a wall and not stop to watch him slide down it. Instead, he turned back to me and extended a hand to help me up. The kids bolted, scuttling like rats through any exit they could find.

'Somebody told me they saw the kids grab a young guy,' Mike bellowed, 'and from the description, had to be you. Why the fuck did you sneak off like that? I'd have got you to the depot safe enough.'

'I couldn't let you,' I said, standing up to him because I had to, not because I thought I had any chance in hell. Even well, Mike could have flattened me. 'Nella was going to talk you into trying to come with me. Shit, that's what these kids wanted. I had to go before that happened.'

Only Jamie, Brock and Greta remained. Jamie had started to leave but Brock grabbed him and held him by one ragged sleeve. Mike turned away from me, half in disgust, to stare at them.

'That right?' he asked. 'You street rats want to go fry in Perth?'

'They're going to push us out,' Greta said in her sharp, clear voice. 'The word's all over the place. The government want to shove us out and pull the city in.'

'Do what?' I asked.

'It's too big. They can't hold it,' Brock said. 'Too many folk. All them what came from your place and other places. You know, over the sea.' He gestured vaguely and I realised suddenly, he couldn't think of any country names, but he knew about all the people from other places, who were piling into the eastern cities. Those cities were in danger

Nightsiders Sue Isle

of breaking under the strain. There was a poem, a Kipling poem, about that which I'd had to memorise at school. It floated through my brain and out again. I couldn't concentrate while Mike and Brock were both yelling.

'So why do they care if you stay here?'

'They're scared of us,' Greta said.

Mike didn't answer for a minute. He looked at me. I could see him wanting to yell that no guy was scared of a little girl, but warring with that was the knowledge of his own anger with me, partly borne of his knowledge that the gang had jumped me the moment I was alone in the night. He had known I couldn't reach the depot safely.

I was cold, I realised, now that I wasn't scared of being killed. Everything I wore was soaked through and that strange, goosepimpled feeling, a deadening, was all over me. That alien feeling was cold.

'Ash!' Mike shook me and it was like being in a collapsing building. 'Oh fuck. Wake up!'

I woke up back in the hospital. They treated me pretty well and didn't say anything about it being my fault that I'd got soaked and chilled and beaten up, right after surgery. They even gave me some probably expensive drugs to help me recover. Dr Bornstein came to see me to make sure I knew that. She was in civvies, her pale hair tied strictly back.

'This is the last time,' she said. 'You have to leave the city as soon as we discharge you. No leeway.'

'Because I got mugged?'

'Because you're out of time and you've brought yourself to the attention of the authorities,' she said. 'I've spoken to

Nation of the Night

some people involved in the, ah, movement of goods between your Perth Nightside and here. There's a truck leaving for the Nightside tomorrow and the trucker has agreed that you can ride with her. Given your injuries, you won't have to help load but she wants you to do some driving. Her name is Sharon Palmer and I'm told she drives a rig named the *Blood Bitch*.' This was said with a distaste which almost made me grin, but I didn't. Probably Bornstein would have thought I was laughing at her for some unknown reason.

All my problems solved with a thump on the head, in a manner of speaking. So why wasn't I happy?

'Um, is Mike around? The orderly who brought me in? I wanted to...'

'I'll pass on your thanks.' She cut the words off as though with a freshly sharpened scalpel. I couldn't ask about Nella and the kids, or about the half-starved boys and the girl who had kicked me in the ribs. I had to go, and perhaps never know. Bornstein took a last look at my chart, nodded and strode out, back to her life.

I met up with Sharon Palmer at the Flagstaff depot. She was a tough, sunburned woman who looked at me with minimal interest and ignored me after saying, 'Get in and belt up.'

As we rolled out of the truck yard, I stared at the grey cliffs of terrace housing and wondered where all the crowds had gone. There were only a few kids playing in the puddles outside the depot gates. Kids always played like that, except in Perth they played in the dustdevils. One of the kids looked up as the *Blood Bitch* rumbled past and ran forwards, unfortunately on the driver's side, so that Sharon Palmer unleashed

Nightsiders   Sue Isle

a surprising string of curses.

It was Emiri! She was shrieking out, 'Ash, Ash, it's me, can you see me, Ash?'

'What's this, your little girlfriend?' Sharon demanded.

'Can I get down for a sec to talk to her, please? She's the daughter of a friend—didn't get a chance to say goodbye.'

'I'm not a lonely hearts club, kid—three minutes!'

I jumped down, just as Emiri cleared the front of the truck. 'Get back on the pavement! What are you doing here?'

'Uncle Mike wanted me and Rafe to watch out for you, only Rafe's arguing with some guys that way.' She pointed up a side street.

'Okay.' I didn't know quite how to express my regrets in eight-year-old terms. 'Um, can you tell him and your mum thanks...'

'He said to tell you we'll come, like Mum said,' Emiri recited, her eyes faraway, clearly dragging the words up from memory. I wondered how accurate she was. 'And that Brock and the other two are with us. Only they're not, they live in some other place,' she told me, focusing on my face again. Behind and above me, Sharon bellowed for me to get my arse back into the truck. 'That girl, Greta, she's teaching me stuff.'

'I bet.' I turned to go. 'Don't listen to Greta too much, okay, your mum's smarter. Tell them, oh hell, I'll look out for them and show you guys around when you get to Perth. And don't tell them the "oh hell".'

Emiri giggled in a way which told me she wasn't going to pay a blind bit of attention to that edit. Then she slid away, back into the knot of kids mucking around on the pavement.

Nation of the Night

By the time I was back in the cab and Sharon was muttering as she put it in gear, there was no sign of Emiri.

In tune with the beast-growling of the large, loaded truck, the words of the old song finally came back to me, some songster's version of Kipling's poem. The careful textbooks teach us the rules of physics but, as Miss Wakeling tried to beat into me for years and years, there were no rules like that for people. There was just us and we had to keep our eyes open and learn. I whispered it quietly, until Sharon demanded to know what I was yabbering about.

'The careful text-books measure
(Let all who build beware!)
The load, the shock, the pressure
Material can bear.
So, when the buckled girder
Lets down the grinding span,
The blame of loss, or murder,
Is laid upon the man.
Not on the steel, the man!'

'I hope you're not going to spew crap like that all the way to the Nightside,' she said.

'Absolutely,' I told her.

Paper Dragons

Itch fell through the roof in a staggering, grabbing dance as the broken tiles gave way. The huge coughing fit that followed told me he wasn't dead, so I didn't immediately plunge down after him. I got as close to the hole as I dared. We'd picked a night close to a full moon, of course, but I still couldn't see anything down it.

'Shani!'

'Yeah, yeah, I'm still up here. You in one piece?'

'I think so. I'm on this pile of paper. Dusty as.' He broke off to cough and sneeze some more.

'Can you get out again, you think?' I shouted, once the sound effects had ebbed away.

'Oh sure. Wall feels rough, lots of footholds. Come on down.'

'I'm making sure I can get back out, fuzzbrain. Can you see any bones around you?'

'Only mine. What's the matter? You're acting like a complete girl.'

That sent me over the edge of the hole. I could judge by his voice that the floor of the house was where it should be, so I only had to hang from my hands on the last decent grip, then drop, twisting neatly so as not to land on Itch. He was lying flat on his back, arms and legs thrown out like a spider who'd lost a few, peering up at me as I stood over him.

'There's a reason for that, Kayama Ichiro! I'm not the one who walked over that weak spot without testing the tiles first. If that's what having balls does for you, I'm glad I am a girl!'

'The first step was okay,' he said weakly, holding out his hand. I took it and pulled him upright, though not as fast as I could have. He mightn't have broken anything but he'd given his head a good whack. My eyes had already adjusted. It still surprises the Elders that we can see this well. Prof Daniel ran some experiments once and found that anyone born five years or so after 2020 had what he called cat-eyes, as well as heat tolerance and some other stuff.

'Sit there for a bit,' I said.

'I'm going to,' Itch answered, which made me worried he was hurt worse than he let on. Regardless, we were here, even if it hadn't happened exactly to plan. When it came to scavenging, medicines were first; then tools, batteries and electricals, clothing and then books. This house had been done over before, but probably right after its owners were evacuated East. At that time there still were regular medicines for sale and shops open and stuff like that. We hoped to find things those early scroungers hadn't bothered with. Itch picked up some of the papers lying around him. 'Printed stuff,' he said. 'Looks like those play sheets Tom and the Troupe use, except theirs are handwritten.'

I went through the rooms quickly. After you've scrounged for almost eight years, you don't need to waste your time.

Paper Dragons

'Itch, I need the rope.' The stairway down to the next level looked sturdy and maybe I'd have risked it if not for Itch's spectacular entry. He made a loud rustling as he moved along the corridor towards me. 'What have you got there?'

'Some of those papers,' Itch said. He sounded defensive but more like his usual self. 'I want to get a proper look at them later.'

'Time to head back soon?' I suggested and he nodded. The distance from the CBD would be one reason why this house hadn't been reclaimed yet. We checked it over anyway, knowing the Elders would want a full report. Plenty of rooms for sleeping and storage but way too many windows, letting in the heat and light so much that the house would be unendurable by day. We found a bathroom with a real tub, sitting on clawed feet, which I admired.

'Not much good without running water,' Itch said wistfully. Ichiro was proof you could miss, or at least want, what you've never had. Maybe he'd never seen running water inside a house in his life but he'd read of how the old folks used to have such things. The way he described cool, clean water running over your skin made me want that wonder as much as he did.

We were both children of the Evac, fourteen years ago, and had been left behind by parents who disappeared into the dust. I'd been born at the beginning of that year and Itch at the end.

We split up, to cover the larger ground floor area more quickly. Itch had a find right away; a box of razors on the floor of the downstairs bathroom. The razors were small enough for us to carry in our shoulderpacks, so we stowed those while we finished our look. The horizon was faintly streaked with light by the time we reached the road and headed back to town. Itch pulled out a few of the papers to examine them.

'It is a play,' he exclaimed. 'Look—there's character names and dialogue and setting notes.'

'So take it to Tom.' I wanted to get going.

That light made me nervous when we were so far from home, and even though Elders had rated the run safe for juniors, that check was several nights old and anyone could have moved into the area since then. Sometimes 'safe for juniors' only means 'they can run faster.'

He let me bully him onwards, clearly only half listening. I could read his mind way better than I could those play sheets. The Players' Troupe, led by Tom Roper, was as much a fixture as anything in our world. They did street theatre, which meant they performed anything they could, any way they could, but they worked hard; as hard as anyone labouring in the shaded farms or rebuilding homes or trying to save lives. If Ichiro wanted to be an actor, he had to prove he could carry his own weight. He brought them every shiny scrap of pretty metal or bright-coloured cloth he found and that was fine. That got him into backstage but not on to the stage. Not yet.

Clear grey light filled the world by the time we were back in Perth CBD. Someone was at the door-flap of our Northbridge building, holding it up just enough to see out and to show us a pale section of face. Our building isn't one of the tall, important-looking ones. The downstairs used to be a shop and the upstairs was storage. It took the Elders months

Paper Dragons

of work to fill in all the holes when they moved in. It was Liane at the door. 'You're late,' she whispered.

'We're fine. Didn't see anybody,' Itch assured her. Next to his shiny black hair and amber skin, Liane looked as pale as a ghost gum, skin and hair almost the same lightness. You couldn't see her eyes in the shadows but they were blue, so washed out they were nearly white. She never went out at all; the other two Elders, Alex and Janine, did any travelling that had to be done. She was portal-guard this day and slept at the entrance, so lightly that any noise would wake her. Itch went in, rustling down the stairs into the sleep lair and I followed him. The others were there; Alex, Janine, Rekha and Kateb, on their thin mattresses. The only light came from the doorway, brighter every minute.

'You kids,' Janine began, 'you're...'

'Late, we know,' I said. 'Liane already said. And we're not. It's only just light outside and we did the house as fast as we could.'

'Don't answer back,' Janine said. That was typical Elder. Didn't matter how good an argument you had; you weren't allowed to say it until you had grey hair, far as I could tell. Itch wasn't bothered. He was pulling the papers out from his pants and piling them neatly by his pallet. Kateb, who was nearest, peered at them, though it wasn't light enough to read.

'Toilet paper?' he wondered politely. Kateb is seventeen and he's the oldest of the kids Janine and Alex adopted. He has black hair like Itch's and brownish skin like mine, but he's not local like me. His folks came here from a place called Iraq, which Kateb says got as hot as Perth does now,

Nightsiders   Sue Isle

only the people learned to live with it.

'It's a play,' Itch said proudly. 'I'm going to take it to Tom. Maybe if he produces it, I can have a part.'

'If he doesn't, I can use the paper,' Kateb yawned. He rolled over on his side and ignored us. Rekha dipped some water out of the big pan that was always kept in the room and passed the dipper to me. 'You must have hurried back,' she said. 'You're still sweating.' That's Rekha, always gentle and polite and smoothing everything over. She can even calm Janine down when she's ready to throttle either Itch or me for something. Rekha is sixteen. She joined us when she was seven and she wouldn't talk for months, not even to Alex, who used to talk to people as a job.

Itch had finished rustling and settled down too, stripping off like the rest of us in preparation to wait out the day. I hoped for some decent sleep. I knew what we'd be doing as soon as night came again.

Tom Roper dubiously accepted the thick, crinkled wad of paper from Itch, who was grinning like an idiot. The whole Troupe was there in the backstage tent, crowded in with the coloured boards and banners and piles of fancy costumes. This was only a rehearsal night, so everybody was fairly laid back. Even Tom was in normal gear, for him; a long skirt in some light material and a cotton shirt. Tom's hair was halfway down his back and tied in a neat French braid. I wished I could do that but then, my hair's shorter than Itch's. You don't want fancy when you scrounge.

Itch started to tell Tom where he found the papers, getting all dramatic about the fall through the roof. Tom tuned him

Paper Dragons

out and began skim-reading the thing. 'This is page seven. Do you have the rest?'

'I can get it!'

Tom raised his brows thoughtfully and passed out pages at random to the others. They'd be keen to read anything new. I watched them laugh and quote bits to one another.

'There's a lot of teenagers in this,' Ash Henderson remarked, finishing a page and turning it over to see if anything was written on the back. 'Some girl who's had a baby and wasn't supposed to, and two boys fighting over another girl.'

'Sounds like Shakespeare,' groaned someone else.

'Have some respect,' Tom growled. Diss anybody but the Bard. 'For your information, Ash; having a child out of wedlock was once considered a Bad Thing.'

'Locked out of what?'

Tom glared, knowing Ash wasn't that ignorant. Ash was nineteen so he was pre-Evac, though he'd been pretty young. He'd also been a girl at the time, which had messed with my head until I worked it through. Ash was a boy in his mind and that was where you were a boy or a girl. I looked at Ash, who was busy reading so didn't see me look. He was dark-haired and slim, not much taller than me and looked younger than his age.

Finally Tom got tired of the racket and yelled for everyone to shut up. He looked down at Itch, who was still standing looking hopeful in the centre of the tent. 'Okay. You get me the rest of this so I can see if it makes sense. You lot, help me count the pages so I can tell Ichiro which pages we need.'

Itch still hadn't asked, so I did it for him. 'Tom?'

Nightsiders   Sue Isle

'Shani?' he asked without looking at me.

'Like you said, there are a lot of kids in this play and not too many of the Troupe are kids. You've got Ash and Minh but 'most everybody else is kind of...'

'Don't say old,' Tom warned me.

'Not suitable for playing teen parts,' I said demurely. 'And Itch—Ichiro's done lots of practice. He puts on plays for us, you know, and he's been to see most of your performances.'

Tom surveyed Itch and then looked back at me. 'I'll think about it. Get me the rest when you can. Tell Janine I'll trade for your time.'

Itch went back to get the papers next sunset, alone because I was on another job. Though I would much rather have been crashing through roof tiles. Instead, I was wasting my entire night setting out chairs for the monthly town meeting. Janine was in charge, which meant no hope of dodging out the door. Even Kateb was there. Rekha had volunteered and she'd also volunteered Kateb and me. Alex got to stay home and housesit this time.

'I heard Liane is coming to this one,' Kateb said to me as he unloaded a stack and handed me the top chair.

'No way. Too much open ground.'

'Yes way. Something's got her stirred up.'

I began setting out the new row. On a good month they would get up to five hundred people at Meeting. It was the most fun many of them ever saw. Janos Duskovich, the Shadow Court Judge, usually ran things.

The meeting place sits up the top of a long hill, not too far from the river, ages away from most of the other reclaimed

96

Paper Dragons

places. We don't use too much of the inside because the roof fell in and it's not safe. Just the hall, where you end up after you climb the front steps and walk far enough in to get away from the sun. It has very high ceilings and pictures of a lot of old guys and women on the walls. Mostly we set up enough chairs to fill the hall and then the people running the meeting stand on the first few stairs of the staircase.

I doubted Liane would make it. A lot of the Elders don't go outside at all. It's like the Evacuation messed up their brains. They didn't want to leave their homes but they couldn't live the way they used to, and they heard so little from the outside world. Ash's housemate Prof Daniel was like that. He'd gone into his squat when the University fired him, so Ash said, and never come out. I wondered why they didn't just go East, but when I asked Ash, since he'd been there, he said they didn't want us any more.

We finished and sat drinking water while we waited for people to show up. Too far to go home and return; that would take until moon-rise and Meeting was supposed to start at nightfall. I wanted to go home anyway—Meeting is boring—but Janine said no. 'You want to meet Drainers?' she asked me.

'In the middle of CBD? Come on, Janine. You think it's okay for Itch and me to go out to the suburb houses.'

'Not okay,' she said. 'Necessary. You like eating, don't you?'

'So do Drainers,' said Kateb and made a hideous slurping sound through his teeth.

People began to come in then so we had to leave the discussion. Rekha and I stood by the entrance with the waterbucket and passed people drinks as they came in. Elders take the heat hard and it's not just because they are Elders. It's like being able to see in the dark; kids have it and they don't.

Tom arrived in something flouncy and pink, followed by most of the Troupe. 'We don't have the Judge tonight,' he announced. 'He drank some bad water, he says, and unless he can preside sitting on a privy, he's not going anywhere. Since this is possibly not in the public interest or the dignity of the office, I've agreed to be his deputy.'

'You bring a totally whole new light to the term "dignity of the office", Mr Roper,' Janine said, sounding resigned. 'I especially like the silver tassels on the hem of that skirt, by the way. Are there any particular orders of business that you know about?'

'Not a thing,' Tom said cheerfully. 'Let's ad lib it, shall we?'

We got half an hour through an 'ad lib' concerning patrol numbers around the city limits when a woman swathed in dark cloth staggered through the door. She had her headscarf lowered so we couldn't see who it was. People surrounded her, trying to calm her and get her to sit down but she tore away from them and pulled the headcloth off. Despite Kateb's warning earlier, we were still shocked to see Liane. She looked about to collapse on the spot but pushed Janine and Rekha away when they tried to help. When she tried to talk, the words slid out in a sort of hiss. Rekha passed Liane a dipper of water and got her to drink it. Tom was still on the stairs, waiting, as was the whole meeting. Finally someone asked Tom, 'Can someone say what Lio's freaked about? She might calm down if we, you know, talk about it?'

Paper Dragons

'Okay,' Tom said, resigned. 'We'll table the thing about increased patrols—can you make a note about that, Minh? Liane, if you want to say something, you've got the floor.'

Liane was calming down some now she was inside and people she knew were close by. She even said 'Thank you' to Rekha and gave her back the dipper. Then she pulled the scarf close around her head again and walked slowly down the path between the chair rows. 'Ichiro brought pages back,' Liane blurted out. 'They're not from a play. I know what they're from. I used to watch it on television when I was a teenager. It was my whole life, around the time my parents put me in the institution. You won't know its name, none of you know any names. Most of you weren't even born!'

I'd never known how old Liane was, only that she was older than Alex and Janine, who were old enough for us to have been their natural kids. I looked around the foyer. Most people here had been small kids at the time of the Evac. There was just a handful like Tom and Alex and Janine. There were more Elders but they were home. They were always home.

'Don't wake it up,' Liane was pleading now, for a wonder loud enough that Janine didn't have to echo. She was turning around to look at people, her headscarf falling back so you saw her ghostly hair and skin, her eyes pale in the light from the torches. 'Those screen stories were so beautiful. Yes, I knew they weren't real, but they pretended everything was so wonderful and you could believe it while you were watching. All around me, everything was starting to die. Everything green turned brown and people who went into the sun got sick and then they went away. They wanted to take me away!'

Nightsiders   Sue Isle

Her voice dropped into sadness but then she laughed, right at me. 'Only children are left and you don't understand anything. You have your little meetings up here in the ruin of the goddamned Parliament! Do you even know what this building was? And you send children to steal from the dead and bring back all that lovely foolishness that should stay sleeping.'

Her voice rose into hissing and squeaking again and Janine hastily put an arm around her and persuaded her away, into the depths of the building. Liane would probably calm down and not even remember what she had said. Tom would, though. He had that look of packing away what he'd heard, so it would be there when he wanted to go over it.

Ash caught up with me halfway down the long hill road, on the bridge, where it crossed over the road far below. I didn't much want to talk to Ash, though usually we got on fine. Right now he was too much one of the Elders. He'd be twenty soon. 'Hey, Shani,' he said. I grunted something and kept walking. 'Is it okay if I come back to your place and talk to you and the others a bit?'

'Itch's going to be tired,' I said.

'Itch will be dancing up and down, if I know him, and Kateb and Rekha haven't been working tonight except for coming to Meeting. I won't take long anyhow.'

Minh, small and looking delicate, walked up beside us. It looked like both of them were coming home with me, like it or not. We didn't talk much. That's not a good idea when walking through the city; you need to keep a lookout. There's maybe two thousand people left here and some of them are seriously strange. We trotted along the old train

100

Paper Dragons

platform as quickly as we could, not looking down at the tracks, where a few folk were moving around; black against dark. Then we were in the open again, walking around the piles of rubble.

Alex answered the door at once as soon as I knocked, but he still looked so worried I knew he'd been hoping it was Liane. 'She's at Meeting,' I told him. 'Janine's looking after her.'

'Thank God. Hi Ash, Minh. Come in and have a drink.' It was fruit juice, for a wonder, oranges squeezed at one of the sheltered farms, I guessed. Itch came up from the underground room and sat with us. Alex lit a candle and set it safely in a dish. 'How'd it go?' he asked, and I knew he wasn't asking about usual business.

'She freaked about the play Itch found,' Ash said. 'She thinks it's going to wake up old things.'

'I've been reading it,' Alex told him. 'Liane is probably right.'

Itch fidgeted. 'It's a play,' he complained. 'So it's about old times, so what? So's all the stuff you guys do. Or did Dunsinane Forest suddenly spring up in Perth CBD?'

'That isn't our own Dreamtime, to borrow an Original word,' Minh said softly. 'This play is.'

Ash's eyes gleamed in the candlelight as he leaned forward in the circle where we sat. 'That's why we have to put it on. Itch, Shani, are you game for that?'

'Why do you want Shani in it?' Itch grumped. 'She's not an actor.'

I could see he didn't mean to be nasty to me. This was his thing and I'd never shown any interest in being a Player.

101

Nightsiders   Sue Isle

'She's a teen,' Ash said patiently. 'I want to ask Rekha and Kateb if they'll join us too. Itch, after we perform the play, Shani and the others will drop out and Tom will have really seen what you can do. You'll have your chance to join the Troupe. Okay?'

'Okay,' he said reluctantly.

'Alex?' Ash looked at our Elder, who was rubbing his stubbly jaw thoughtfully. 'If Liane finds out we're doing this she's going to freak.'

'She'll have to find out in the end,' Alex pointed out.

'No she won't. She doesn't leave your place and if none of your family tells her...' Ash trailed off. I guess he could see the gaping holes in his own logic. 'Anyway, can you not tell anyone right now?'

'Why can't you leave this to Tom?' Alex asked. 'Itch says he's interested in putting the thing on. Probably Tom would be just as keen on having Itch and the rest of this lot perform. It feels like you're sneaking around behind his back and that doesn't make me too comfortable.'

'He'll know before we put it on,' Ash said.

'You'll tell him?' Alex pushed.

'I'll tell him.' Ash took a moment or two to say it, rather unhappily, and Alex nodded.

'Okay.'

Itch was really good. He didn't like it that I was so surprised but he got me back when it was my turn front and centre. Learning lines wasn't my thing. Worst was that Itch knew my lines along with his. Second worst was that we had to rehearse by day when nobody else was around. We used a

102

Paper Dragons

place near Ash's lair, but we still had to get there and back and stay awake while any normal person was asleep. 'We' meant Itch, me, Ash, Minh and a couple of kids Minh knew, who, like Itch, helped out backstage. Kateb and Rekha had refused the chance for theatre stardom.

'You think Liane won't catch onto something if all four of us are heading out at crazy hours and won't say where and what for?' Kateb had said.

'Shani, you have to pay more attention to how your character thinks,' Ash told me now, at our second rehearsal. 'Brittany is this airhead beach princess whose only thought is nailing Aiden. Can't you at least try to look like Itch is actually this gorgeous hunk you're lusting after, so that when your boyfriend walks in you show guilty shock instead of mild surprise?'

I choked back a giggle and Itch sighed. 'Maybe if he stood on something?' I suggested. The fact that I had to look down at Itch made the illusion kind of difficult to maintain. He wouldn't be bad looking in a couple of years, but not yet. Ash was playing the part of the other guy in this threesome but was also directing, so he dropped in and out of his role as required. It looked easy when Ash did it but my head was hurting over the whole business. I didn't know what a beach princess was but I'd had enough of sounding like an idiot so didn't ask.

'Try it again from when Brittany finds Aiden in the games room,' Ash said.

'How are we going to present that?' Minh asked suddenly from where she was sitting against a wall pitted with breaks and lines. 'Prof Daniel said a games room was full of toys

103

Nightsiders   Sue Isle

that used electricity and music and bright lights. We can't
do this like Shakespeare and just toss off a line or two to set
the scene.'

'Why not?' Ash retorted.

'Well, Shakespeare's stuff was meant to be like that. The
audiences expected a bare stage like—like this room.' Their
voices were rising. 'I've been reading this play and it was
crowded. Just like it was somebody's real house and—and
playroom or whatever. When the scene called for the protags
to be arguing on the beach, they went to the real ocean and
recorded everything.'

Daniel had run us through the concept of television. It
sounded boring; making everything tiny, like a very small
playhouse in a box.

'They had so much stuff,' Minh concluded unhappily. 'Cold air and freezers for food and fancy clothes for
everything.'

'And that's why you're rehearsing in stealth?' Tom Roper
asked.

I squeaked in shock and Itch sort of froze on the spot.
Ash crushed the pages he was waving about in his hand.
Tom walked in—stage centre—to stand in front of Ash.
Tom looked weird and it took me a moment to see why. He
was wearing ordinary pants and a loose shirt in the pale
dull colours everybody wore. His hair was tied back in a
ponytail to keep it away from his face and neck. Though it
couldn't have felt good to stand in front of that look, Ash
did his best. 'This is only our second run through,' he said.
'I didn't want to bring it to you until I was sure we had
something.'

104

Paper Dragons

'You could still have used our rehearsal space,' Tom said. I had just long enough to consider the fact that I was actually checking Ash out before Tom turned on the rest of us. 'Minh, Gregory, Chandra—out. Shani and Ichiro, you had better go home.' I saw that Itch was actually disappointed at not being lumped in with the rest of the Players. He didn't move for a moment, so I grabbed his hand and pulled him out of the room. Behind us, we heard Tom's voice deepen into lecture mode. Itch shivered.

'It's not that bad,' I said, trying to convince myself we weren't leaving Ash to be slaughtered. 'He's raised Ash from when he was five or something. It's like when Alex or Janine yells at us.'

'But I found the play. It's my fault.'

'What fault? We find all kinds of stuff. We couldn't know that Liane was going to freak about it.'

'It's not just her. If it was, Tom would already be producing.'

Itch was still hanging on to my hand and I used the link to tug him towards shade—a big building with 'Newspaper House' on its side. Hard to think of a whole building being used to make newspaper but there you are. There sure is a lot of it around the place.

'We ought to hide,' Itch said. 'He told us to go home and he'll be mad that we didn't.'

'He said it was a good idea,' I pointed out. 'He can't tell us because we don't belong to him,' I pointed out.

We slid belly-down in the dry grass when Tom emerged. He walked away without looking in our direction. When Ash came out, he walked right over to us and slid down against

105

Nightsiders   Sue Isle

the wall, as though his legs had given way.

'What'd he say?' Itch demanded eagerly. 'Did he belt you?'

'Get real, Ichiro. I'm nineteen, not nine.'

'He did something, though,' Itch stated and I wondered why he was so sure. Ash did look a bit funny, like he'd had a bad shock.

'Kind of,' Ash said and looked at us thoughtfully. 'Do you guys think you can be ready for stardom in a week?'

'Huh?' I asked.

'Tom told me,' Ash explained with careful clarity, 'that if I'm so sure I know better, that our premiere performance is to be next week. He'll postpone *Much Ado About Nothing*, which he seemed to think a really funny joke for some reason. We get the facilities. We get Gregory, Minh and whatever stagehands we need. He's going to make sure the entire city is watching.'

'The old people won't come,' Itch said softly. 'Liane will have the bad dreams again.'

Ash still looked worried, staring into some distance that wasn't the brilliant, burning day directly in front of our patch of shadows. 'Tom was really strange. He said he hoped we were ready for what we wake.'

We rehearsed every hour we could, every night that week. Itch and I had jobs piling up so high that we'd be Elders ourselves before we got another night off. Alex and Janine weren't happy and Liane didn't say a word to us the whole time.

On performance night, as soon as the temperature dropped enough to move, we began to set up. About then, time began to run strangely. I helped Gregory organise the

106

Paper Dragons

costumes and it felt only minutes had passed before Minh came in to say we had to get changed. I couldn't remember a thing as we helped each other into the funny checked dresses that were our characters' 'school uniforms'. I headed for the entrance but walked straight into Greg instead.

'Ash!' he whispered loudly, 'there's a huge mob out there and they're old people!'

Ash, in costume and jumping around doing a dozen jobs, gripped Greg's shoulder and pulled him towards us, out of the possible view of any audience. 'Don't be dumb. They're here to watch, not make trouble.'

'Some of them look pretty intense,' Greg shot back, but he headed on to the back of the tent. My legs felt weirdly heavy.

'You're on, Shani,' Ash murmured behind me, and I was. I walked out there alone, trying not to stumble. I didn't think I could remember my own name, let alone my lines. I was scared I'd fall into the backdrop, with its colourful drawing of the inside of an old-times house. Big furniture, book-shelves, a TV, and other electrical stuff. I had to walk forward to the mark on the paving, start talking there and then turn around when Itch ran after me. *Brittany*, I thought hard, *I'm Brittany, high school chick in the 2000s, coming home from school. Parents are out at their jobs, my boyfriend is stalking me.*

Then I saw the audience. Greg had said there were a lot of people, but this crowd overflowed the half-circle of stone steps around us. They crowded so close that we hardly had the minimum performance area on the flat paving. They stood above the steps and perched on the crumbled walls

107

of the buildings there. Barely three steps from me, in the first row, were seven or eight people I didn't know. This is a bizarre thing when you live in a community of only two thousand, rattling around a city which once held two million and some. I didn't know them and they were the oldest people I had ever seen.

Liane, her headscarf pushed halfway back, was the youngest and I knew she was in her forties at least. Some of these folks had smoky-white or grey hair, and skin as wrinkled as crushed paper. They were so pale that they could never have walked outside in the sun. On either side of Liane were a couple of women so frail that a desert wind would have blown them to sand. They couldn't run from any threat. Some of these people had probably had to be carried here, to sit outside on hard stone in a burning night and hear words that were fifty years old. Their soft murmur of conversation was stilling and I realised only a few moments had passed since I had walked onstage. All of them stared at me and in Liane's eyes there was challenge.

And I became Brittany. It was weird. I knew I was still me but I seemed to be someone else as well; a girl who thought about clothes and boys as though they were everything. She was worried about who liked who and who would find out. Trouble with her studies. Parents who made rules. To her, there never was an Evacuation. She lived in a cooler, richer world and she never even noticed. More than that. She was those old people and they had been her and her friends. So finally, while I said Brittany's words, a part of me knew why the old people had tried to stop this.

Paper Dragons

My character wasn't in the last scene. That was a violent argument between 'Aiden' and 'Jai', Itch and Ash's characters. So I watched, hidden backstage, while they played out the roles of two boys, older than me, who had nothing more to worry about than a girl who liked both of them. Words blew out like dust storms, over the crowd who were scarily silent now.

'She's my girlfriend,' Itch/Aiden snapped. 'She'll never be yours and we want you out of here!'

We didn't have music or theme songs. Ash had said that wouldn't matter. The old people seemed to wait for something more, though, but as Itch faced them and bowed, everyone applauded. Quickly I joined the others to run forward and bow also.

'Oh no,' Itch muttered very softly and I looked. Liane was standing up and so were her friends. Some younger people behind them helped the very frail ones to stand. I waited for Liane to start yelling. Then I saw that they were crying. I could have handled shouting. I took a quick look around, hoping for Tom or some of the other adult Players, but none of them stepped forward. For good or bad, this was ours. Tom had told Ash that.

More people were standing now until the entire audience was on its feet. They'd stopped clapping, which I found deeply creepy. Were we that bad or that good?

'I remember the Evacuation,' Liane called out, louder than I'd ever heard her. 'They never asked, you know? People from the cities in the East came here and herded us on to planes and buses. They powered down the city and closed

109

Nightsiders   Sue Isle

doors behind them. We learned to live without them, those
of us who chose to; stayed away from the search parties. We
made our own world here even though those people didn't
believe we could.'

'But we hide,' said a man in a heavy coat. He was skinny
and silver-haired like one of the half-dead trees which grow
in the streets. 'We've stopped choosing.'

'Our families and friends look after us,' said another
woman.

'You're scared,' Ash said. I jumped; he was right next to
me and at first I thought he was talking to me.

Then I heard him raise his voice, clear and carrying
without shouting, the way a trained Player knows how to do.
'You were too old to learn to live in the heat like we have. You
can't see properly in the dark but you've never told us why
you never went over to the East where it's maybe a bit cooler,
where the infrastructure still exists and there's a network of
settlements that can support each other, not just one city.'

'If we went, we'd be refugees,' Liane went on. 'There were
so many from other countries shown to us on screens. Whole
nations on the move, starving, living in camps. We were
always better than that; don't you see? I used to host online
interactive shows for a job. People listened to me—they
wanted to be like me. That made me a celebrity back then,
you know. And the East isn't so much better off. It was very
hard for them to absorb nearly three million people from
this city and its surrounds. They don't want any more of us.
You know that!'

She took a step forward, joining us on the stage rather
than staying with the crowd and for some reason, looked

110

Paper Dragons

at me. 'We're out now and we don't plan to give up again. You'll see some changes.'

She nodded to us and began to thread her way through the people, out and back towards our home. As though that had been a signal, the great crowd began to disperse, still in silence. The compulsion to stand there suddenly disappeared and I bolted back around the screen into the tent, desperate to get the stupid checked dress off and my own clothes back on so I could get out of here. Itch, the idiot, was starting to yabber with Ash and Minh and everyone about how terrific it had been and Ash said something about the fantastic result and we'd gotten an entire generation back and he couldn't wait to talk it over with Daniel.

Had Prof Daniel been here? I hadn't seen him. I managed to get changed by one candle amid a mess of everyone's things and sneak out the back before anyone could grab me and make me stay for the 'cast party' Ash had told us would happen. They were all crazy. I knew for dead sure now the last thing I wanted to be was a Player. I wasn't sure what I did want but I'd have it, whatever it was.

The Schoolteacher's Tale

Shani was married in the autumn. She asked me to be her attendant Elder, but I wasn't too sure I wanted the honour. She'd only just graduated from my classroom, so she was certainly still in her teens and her intended was even younger. Teenagers these days. They never spend time living together to see if everything works out, no, they have to be properly hitched. In a city with so few people remaining that we're more like a small village among the ruins, the teens have gone crazy about propriety.

Not that crazy, as it turned out.

'The baby's due in six months,' Shani told me, standing to one side as I made inventory of the school cupboard, by the last half hour of available sunlight, checking the supplies of chalk, pencils, paper and other oddments. Somebody would have to scavenge for more soon, if no trucks came our way from the east. Some said the government was trying to flush the last few lost souls from Perth but others said that was nonsense: Ash hadn't been allowed to stay in Melbourne, two years before.

'Would you ask your folks to come see me?' I asked her. 'I need someone to go on a supply run.'

113

'Yes, Miss Wakeling.'

'Ellen, Shani. You're out of school, you're getting married. I think you count as a grownup now, so it's Ellen.'

The young girl grinned with pleasure, looking even younger. She'd always been a nice kid, attractive, with brown hair and unusually clear skin, quick at school skills and adept at Nightside survival.

It's strange that the young folk don't seem curious about what happens beyond our borders. They're only a little bit curious about the other cities, not that Ash has ever talked much about his trip. There's a vague assumption that those places are in the same situation as us. 'Those places' being the countries and cities they can remember from geography class at school. The mindset bothers me, even if nobody under twenty-five cares. We have a very few scratchy phone lines around the city, generally used by the seniors, but the technology of the twenty-first century is now out of our reach.

I teach school as though we were in the nineteenth century, or earlier. They learn by repetition, mostly because there aren't that many books and we need to take care of those we do have, not parcel them out to a mostly-indifferent pack of teens. I teach reading, spelling, maths, geography, history and biology, the last of which consists of teaching them what's safe to eat. For that, we generally link up with one of the Aboriginal communities and have some of their people take the children out with them. In return, we supply them with some of our vegetable produce from the covered farms and sometimes medical care. When we have bandages and antibiotics.

The Schoolteacher's Tale

The children are in my care until they reach the age of thirteen or fourteen and go on to their adult lives. Truly, there's no reason to keep them inside the walls any longer. The occasional maths genius is passed on to Prof Daniel, for teaching in return for whatever barter arrangement they can come up with. Those who show a flair for acting or recitation or even sewing are passed on to Tom Roper's Troupe. There isn't a whole lot more we can do with them and we wouldn't be able to hold them against their will. Shani, for instance, became a very accomplished scrounger, often working with her now-fiancé, Ichiro Kayama. There's a university still, but that's more a separate community than a place of advanced learning. They still have lecturers and students and classes, but those things don't seem to mean what they would have to someone of my generation.

'Are you alright, Miss Ellen?'

I jumped. I'd honestly forgotten that Shani was still standing beside me. They used to put people like me in 'retirement homes' where our meals were made for us and we slowly marinated in front of television sets. I'm not sure what the Nightside community is going to do for us, if anything. Our other oldest folk are at least ten years younger than me and I'm in my late seventies.

'Yes, Shani, sorry. The aged mind wanders. Where do you plan to hold the ceremony?'

'At our new place,' she said. 'We've staked out a house at the Edge, so we're going to have the smoke ceremony there.'

The Edge? That could mean anything and anywhere. 'How far from here?' I asked.

115

Nightsiders   Sue Isle

Shani frowned. She'd been good with kilometres and travel times at school but now she said, 'An hour or two, I think, in the cool.' She meant at night, of course, and it wasn't cool. Just bearable to travel. 'You don't have to worry, though, Miss—uh—Ellen. We'll bring you out the night before and you can stay over.'

'What about your parents?' A lot of seniors didn't like to go outside unless they had to. Shani's parents, of course, weren't that kind and they weren't her blood relatives. They'd been counsellors before the Evacuation. Now they were foster parents to as many feral and damaged children as needed them. Both Shani and Itch had spent their lives under the roof of Alex and Janine.

'I don't know,' she said quietly. 'They're not sure they can leave the kids and the kids don't want to come to the Edge.'

This Edge again. I shrugged a little; there wasn't much I could do. 'All right, Shani. You'll come and get me evening before at my house, yes?'

She grinned again. 'In person, Miss Wakeling,' and was gone. I decided the Ellen thing probably wasn't going to work.

The sun was still up when the teens arrived with my transport. I was already in my long-sleeved gown, so I just had to put my shady hat on. I glanced around as I stepped into the street, automatic reflex even now, to check whether the neighbours were watching. The hot breeze blew the dust and rattled stones, but this suburb, once called 'inner-city', was quiet. We were past the deadliest of the heat but not yet to the cooler times when folk stirred themselves to work on their homes or visit with their neighbours in the light.

The Schoolteacher's Tale

I regarded the transport. It was a donkey cart. They must've gotten the donkey from an outer farm; there certainly weren't any hereabouts. If there ever had been, they'd been eaten by the short-sighted. The cart had begun life as a trailer designed to be pulled behind a car, but the wheels now were wooden, bumpy but long-lasting, and the traces were metal rods from a source I didn't recognise. Shani and Itch were both there, together with a young Asian girl I recognised from the street actors, and from my classes a year or so back. 'I'm Minh, Miss Wakeling,' she said in answer to my no doubt confused expression. She took my bag and hoisted it aboard, while Itch walked beside me and put his arm around my back to heave me up. Then he scrambled up beside me. Shani passed him the reins before she and Minh climbed into the back of the cart.

'No seatbelts,' I blurted, of the driver's bench where I sat in state beside Itch, who laughed.

'Ed doesn't go fast enough for that,' he said, 'but you better hang on, it's pretty bumpy.'

It was. The cart rattled and shuddered constantly, jarring my teeth until I was afraid the remaining ones would be loosened. Yet despite the discomfort I was excited, probably beyond all reason. I hadn't travelled more than the length of a street or so, or around a block of half-ruined high rises, for more than fifteen or twenty years. Now those familiar buildings, the safer ones occupied by groups of people preparing to rise and go about their nighttime lives, fell behind me as Ed's reluctant walk carried us outwards. My mind had held the memory of the city as it had been when I was the age of these children, before the phrase 'climate change' became

Nightsiders   Sue Isle

as much a cliché as grim truth. I remembered the city as it was before the Evac, before the bombings, before the 'flu pandemic which did for flesh and blood what the terrorist attacks had done for our city.

The road taken by our donkey and cart led north, through suburbs which were partly colonised by our people who had moved out of the CBD over the last five years or so. This was still Northbridge, whose heart was our home, but as we moved, the surroundings became more dilapidated, the road more cluttered with junk; dead cars, household goods, even bodies. It was also darker; as the sun set, no fires burned in homes to give light or create the smells of cooking.

'It's all right, Miss Wakeling,' Shani whispered at my ear. 'We've got a pass; we went through today to do the call. No one's going to attack us.'

The teenaged girl thus reassures the fidgety, seventy-six year old woman. I had little idea what she was talking about, how calling out earlier today could guarantee a 'standing down' of the more feral folk who lived here. She was correct, however; we trundled on unmolested, the length of Beaufort Street into the suburb of Mount Lawley and then a turn onto a road now nameless, with not even a post to mark its identity. The silly little divisions meant nothing now, of course. The groups of folk took and held whatever area of land, houses and workshops and gardens, that they could. Shouting broke out to our left, far enough away that I didn't panic, but I did grab the seat harder. Itch drew Ed the donkey to a temporary halt and Minh scrambled down to go to his head and make sure he was all right.

The Schoolteacher's Tale

'Have a drink, Miss Wakeling,' Shani said and passed me a bottle. Minh climbed back on to the cart and we went on. We travelled for more than an hour, perhaps two. Now we were alongside the railway line, its tracks clean and undamaged here, by chance. Back in the city, the underground line had been destroyed very early on by a single bomb and never rebuilt. The children called it the Broken Line and forgot that trains had ever run on it. Often they didn't believe me when I told them.

'How much further?' I asked Shani, hearing the childish echo, my brother and myself bored during a family car trip. *Are we nearly there yet?* The suburb around me was now completely strange, though I must have been here as a child and young adult, in the '20s at least, when the trains still ran and there was petrol for the cars. There were native trees, apparently alive, though it was hard to determine their health by night, and more vegetation than I would have expected. Open areas were covered by shrubs and trees reached upwards, their branches tangling with the dead power lines. Before anyone could answer, I continued, 'How will you ever make this journey constantly, to get to market or for books and schooling, when you need to?'

'We won't be doing it a lot,' Itch said, glancing at me for politeness, though he quickly returned his attention to Ed and the road. 'There are some folk going to be settling near us and we'll be growing stuff. We'll come in to trade but it won't be like every day.'

'What about medical care,' I said weakly. There were medical people remaining, a blend of doctor and nurse and

119

Nightsiders   Sue Isle

midwife and dietician. They lacked a great deal of materials but what they could do was much better than nothing or teenage guessing. 'And won't you be at risk from tribes?'

'That's why we're doing the smoke ceremony,' Shani said patiently. 'The Elders will be attending, they're special guests.'

My back ached and my behind was sore from the hard bench, the rattling and the uncomfortable posture with nothing to lean on. My hand ached with the wish to slap sense into these children, to yell out that they should turn around and take me home, that I didn't want to be involved in this ridiculous game any more.

'You're our Elder,' Shani continued. 'We knew you wouldn't be scared of travelling so far.'

'You're entirely welcome, my dear,' I told her.

At some point we had to leave the road, which had several donkey-and-cart sized holes broken in it, and travel along the bicycle path, which was more or less clear. Forage parties did come out this far and some of them even rode bicycles.

'Hold it right there,' a quite young-sounding man shouted at us, from the looming shadowy shelter of a rather elegant old hotel. 'There's a crossbow on youse!'

I hardly had time to feel frightened before Itch called back. 'Wedding party,' he yelled. 'We called through!'

'Oh yeah,' said the man who had yelled. 'Thanks for the sheep.'

'You're welcome.'

'Any more coming through?'

'No, we're it. We got to take this lady back, though, tomorrow night.'

'She'll be right.'

120

The Schoolteacher's Tale

We clopped on.

'Were they Drainers?' I asked.

Sometimes I wondered if the Drainers were no more than a scary story and if so, what sort of people had dreamed them up.

'No, just normal,' Itch said. 'There's about ten of them live in the Pen—you know, that hotel.'

Conversation lapsed, except for murmurs between the girls behind me. When I looked back, I saw them both watching behind and around us. Call or no call, they were being as careful as they could.

We got there at last. My sense of time is quite good and I estimated we had been travelling for at least three hours. Minh jumped down as we arrived in a laneway beside a house and led Ed away to his rest. The first surprise was that we wouldn't be sleeping inside. Tired and achy and upset, I didn't greet this with particular delight.

'We can't live in the house until the smoke ceremony clears out the spirits,' Shani said. 'Folk could have died in there. We found bones.'

'I trust you cleared them out. Bones, not spirits.'

'Of course we did, Miss Wakeling, but nobody can go in there until after the ceremony and our wedding tomorrow. We've got a really comfortable bed for you in the tent and we'll all be around so it's safe. We've got the lane closed off behind the house and folk patrolling. Have some soup and you'll feel better.'

The tribals arrived with a good deal of noise, around dawn. I peered out of my tent in time to see Shani standing

121

alone in front of the house, facing an elderly Aboriginal woman. Both her companions and Shani's friends were standing well back. The women ringed the old woman and Shani but the men were further back, quite obviously pretending nothing was going on. Shani was in her ordinary cotton skirt and blouse, rather ragged, and the old woman looked even more disreputable. In her right hand she held a smoking branch. Green leaves had been wrapped around it, topped with a damp cloth tied in a knot, so that a tremendous amount of smoke and only a little flicker of flame poured forth.

After a mutter from the old woman, Shani extended her right hand and took the branch. They walked into the house together and soon smoke poured from the open windows and doorway. A mass shout rose up from the women and I found myself scrambling to my feet in the doorway of my tent.

'Let me help you up, Miss Wakeling.' It was Itch, his voice so close that I cried out and nearly fell over. His hand closed under my elbow and bore me up. It was a good thing he held on, because following the shouting from the women, all the men rushed forward, surrounding the house and banging big sticks—spears?—on the ground.

'Now what's going on?' I demanded.

'The house is the women's area, so they've made any evil spirits leave and once they're outside, the hunters frighten them some more so they go right away,' Itch explained. Everyone was shouting now and whether or not it was English, I couldn't tell. 'Are you okay to come meet the Elders? It's part of the thing.'

The Schoolteacher's Tale

I waved my free hand and he led me forward. Shani and the old woman emerged from the house, the smoke stick still, well, smoking. My eyes began to water and I held my breath in an effort not to cough. The Aboriginal Elder took my hands and said something in her own language, then added in English, 'The sleeping place is clean now, it'll be a good place.'

Her appearance startled me. From her greying-black hair and the identification of her group as tribals, I had expected, I suppose, a more purely Aboriginal appearance, but her weathered skin was quite fair, her face even freckled. She had, I thought, equal inheritance from original and invaders. Itch moved me on to meet the others, a man in his fifties, at a guess, and a group of men and women young adult to middle-aged. More surprises. The elderly man was sandy-haired and his face had also a distinctly Asian cast. Among the younger people were quite a few variations from Asian to a man with reddish dreadlocks.

Itch and Shani's friends mingled among the visitors in the yard, as the sun rose. They brought out food and water to share. There was dried meat and vegetables, including some plant matter quite foreign to me, supplied by the tribal visitors. I looked for Itch at one point but he was gone from my side. Time had jumped, the way it does now and then for me. I saw him in the middle of the backyard, hand in hand with Shani, standing in front of the male and female Elders. There was no formal exchange of vows, only a brief murmur I couldn't make out and then shrieks from some of Shani's girlfriends. That simply, the two were married.

Itch and Shani were shepherded into the house by their friends, who stopped at the threshold, shouting

123

encouragement—or worse—as the newlyweds went in. Everyone else kept partying, though I withdrew to a shady tree as the heat built up. Minh came over with a mug of water for me. Behind her were the middle-aged man and elderly woman who had been in charge of the ceremonies.

'This is Mag,' Minh said, indicating the woman, 'and her nephew, Albert. This is our teacher, Ellen.'

Despite the use of my first name and theirs, almost certainly not their real names, Minh spoke with more formality than I'd ever heard. She even seemed a bit nervous as everyone sat down on the ground, watching each other. Around us, people had moved away and begun to settle in available shade, the loud voices quietening, magpies settling at last to rest.

As I watched them, I began to understand that the marriage had been, not the point of this journey, but the pretext. Mag's face was so creased with wrinkles it was hard to decipher her expression, but I felt more relaxed under her attention than I had until now. 'You're the oldest of the folk in the city, right?' she asked me.

'I think so,' I answered carefully. 'I know some in their sixties but I haven't talked to anyone my age or older since the Evac.'

She nodded as though I'd confirmed something they already knew. 'And since then, my people been in the bush area and yours been in their city. That's got to stop. They've done okay till now but they aren't gonna make it if we don't mix it up. Some of us got to go in, some of you got to come out.'

'Why are you asking me?' Even to myself, I sounded

The Schoolteacher's Tale

whiny, nothing like a diplomat. 'There are Aboriginal people in the city area, aren't there? There always were…'

'Not since your Evac,' said Albert. 'We come and got 'em. We're the folk who stayed on country,' he added.

I shouldn't have felt bad for not realising. We had withdrawn to the CBD, made a refuge and grown farms under cover from the sun. Certainly people of all races had travelled around, come to market and gone again.

'You're their eldest,' Mag told me.

I'm their schoolteacher, I wanted to say. That saves me the scrounging for food and some of the discomfort and the injuries they experience, but it also means there isn't anyone to replace me. There are some people who could, given more training, but not yet.

'These kids, they come to the Edge,' she added, nodding towards the house to show she meant Shani and Itch. 'They're in the tribe now, but they're going to stay in this place and make it theirs. They'll have the baby in a few months. You got to come around with us and talk to your people, the ones in the middle and the other ones, the ones who don't live with you.'

Drainers? The people holed up in the old Peninsula Hotel. Maybe others who had dropped off the edge of the world.

'I'm sorry, I don't think that's possible,' I said carefully. 'I have teaching responsibilities. You know I teach the children?'

'They don't need your school no more,' Albert said.

That made me angry. 'You can decide for your own, but these children need to know something of their world! They

125

need to know how to read, write and figure numbers, so that they can understand how the world should work and how one day they can reclaim what's fallen away…'

Albert was getting up. He held out both hands to his aunt to steady her to her feet. She smiled down at me. I expected some 'Elder' last words but there was only the smile and Albert's serious look.

'What did I say?' I wailed to Minh once they were out of earshot.

She looked more confused than I felt. 'I don't know. Did they want you to join their tribe and travel with them? That's a bit funny, isn't it?'

'With my hips, it's a joke,' I muttered. 'Minh, what else is happening here? Would it be really rude for me to ask to go home?'

Minh smiled, humouring the old lady, but I was too rattled to care. 'This evening. It's too much for the donkey, to make him work again today before dark.'

Maybe it was, but within an hour, heat or not, every one of the tribals had taken his or her leave.

Minh and her friend Gregory, another of the players, took me home in the donkey cart that evening.

I should have been too exhausted to be restless but found myself out on the street for my usual walk anyway. A light breeze was blowing, carrying the smell of the rare promise of rain. A few drops fell on my face and I waited, but there were no more. I moved slowly, hoarding my strength but glad to ease the stiffness from the cart ride. I moved straight along my street towards the city centre, as we still called it, the Northbridge hub around which most of us lived.

The Schoolteacher's Tale

The largest buildings were the museum, the art gallery, the contemporary arts school and the state library. That was what they had been. Only a few of us remembered that now. Some of their rooms were still occupied, but by small groups or clans. Some roofless areas were now barter markets or farms, with shadecloth stretched over to protect the plants. I knew one family who bred rabbits in one of the art gallery's chambers and made a good enough living by selling them for fur and meat so that they didn't need to scrounge for supplies. That wasn't where I was headed, though, even though I was hungry enough to think of it. I wasn't sure where I needed to go.

'Miss Wakeling!' I'd nearly been asleep on my feet but the shout from a passing group of young people made me jump awake. 'Did you go to the wedding? How was it?'

I had no idea who it was. My sight had diminished, along with the rest of me. I had none of the uncanny senses of the young. They were only blurs in the darkness, with no street lights or building lights to reveal them. No doubt they had been my students—they had all been my students—but beyond that I was clueless. Still, so far as I knew, there'd been only one wedding today. 'Oh yes. Yes, I did. There was quite a crowd and some tribals came—they had a smoke ceremony to cleanse the house and then a party.'

'Sounds great. I wish I could have got there,' the young man called again and then they moved on, jostling and laughing with each other. A few moments later, I got to the next occupied house to mine. I was fairly far out along Beaufort Street but I had resisted moving when everyone decided to relocate closer to the hub.

127

'Davy!' I called outside the window. 'Jennifer!'

The window slid up noisily and someone leaned out. 'Hello, Ellen. We're well.'

With no infrastructure of city to protect us, us was all we had. So we checked on our friends, particularly the elder of us, the same as Davy would knock on my door if he passed on his way to Weld Square. Jennifer, appearing beside Davy, asked, 'Did you go to the children's wedding, Ellen?'

I repeated what I'd said to the young man. 'They're hardly children now, Jen. Shani will have her own baby by the end of winter.'

'She's too young,' Jennifer said. Her hair was nearly white, though she was at least eight years my junior. I could see it falling untidily as she shook her head. Jen had a lot of health problems but along with her husband, she had stubbornly refused to be evacuated. They rarely left their own house and garden these days. They had grown children who had gone East but there was no contact, could be none.

'Things are different now,' was all I could think of to say. In my world, Shani would indeed have been too young, as would have been Itch, but now, now they were not children. 'I'm going to the centre. Do you need anything?'

'No—we had a supplies visit this morning.'

I said goodbye and moved on, knocking at two other homes where I spoke to the elderly occupants. As I reached the tall structure of the museum, the newest of the big buildings, on impulse I turned left instead of right, which would have taken me to the red paved 'courtyard' between the large buildings of our settlement. Turning left took me past several old buildings, all three to five storeys high. They had been

The Schoolteacher's Tale

damaged by bombing and the normal ravages of years and we weren't able to rebuild them. People still lived in them, though. I got to the one I sought and regarded it, wondering if I was fidgety enough to climb five flights of stairs in order to talk to somebody.

I knocked and had to wait a few moments for the front door to be unbolted and a vague shape to appear. 'Hi, Miss Wakeling,' said yet another anonymous young voice. 'It's Charisse. I'm on door. Did you want somebody?'

'Well, I was hoping to speak to Daniel but it's not urgent.' Only urgent would get the Professor down the stairs and this close to the outside world.

'He was wanting to talk to you too,' Charisse said. She went back into her hide, under the stairwell, and brought out a lit lantern with an air of triumph. It was a candle fitted into a sealed holder, but enough to chase the dark back. Charisse was somewhere in her early twenties, with a ragged fall of brown hair that hid most of her face. 'Hang on, I'll get some carriers.'

I stood listening to her thud up the stairs, calling out and banging on doors. This produced several resigned-looking young males who presented themselves within a few minutes at the doorway, made a clasp of their hands and carried me, effectively if not very elegantly, up the flights to the very top landing. 'Give us a yell when you want to get down,' one said and they dispersed.

Daniel must have been on his own, because after he called out in reply to my hail, I had another wait while he got to the door. If Ash had been home, he'd have opened it before my carriers had deposited me on the landing. He. It's funny,

129

Nightsiders   Sue Isle

I had the most trouble with that child's insistence on being
male. My first memories are of a slim, stubborn little girl,
but now it feels as though Ash was never anything else but
the young man he is.

Finally the door opened and the Professor beckoned me
in. He was in his usual outfit of cotton pants and shirt, once
called trackies. Winter attire. Though Daniel doesn't look
it, I've had the feeling for a long time that he's older than
he lets on. To have been a university lecturer, one supposes
he would have to have been in his mid-twenties at least. The
formal structure of the last university broke up in the '30s;
whatever they have now is purely a grassroots agreement
between the survivors.

Then I saw I'd been wrong about him being alone. Two
people sat very quietly amid the crowded furnishings and
materials in the main room. Daniel rubbed his leg—arthritis,
he says—and made his way slowly back to his battered
armchair.

Mag was sitting in the other 'good' chair and Albert was
perched on a wooden crate.

'Don't you dare say, 'What kept you?'' I warned. Daniel
and I are both from the era of television.

'Well, we were waiting,' he said mildly. 'Mag and Albert
saw you start out along Beaufort ages ago.'

I was glad no one was claiming it was magic. There were
enough odd and uncomfortable things happening around
the Nightside without that. I settled into one of the straight
chairs, not so relaxing but it held me up. 'So if this is a town
meeting, where are the others?'

'I've talked to them,' Daniel said. 'So have my friends.'

130

The Schoolteacher's Tale

He nodded at Mag and Albert. 'And it's not exactly town meeting, I wouldn't be trying to get any changes happening without the others.'

And this way you don't have to leave the building to go to the old Parliament, I thought. He smiled as though he heard me anyway, but I knew that wasn't magic either. We've just known each other a damn long time. 'So let's cut to the chase. What do the three of you want me to do?'

'Teacher exchange,' Daniel said and looked at Mag.

'I'll come teach your kids while you're gone,' she said. 'Al will look after you and you'll look after my folk. We got stuff the others need to know, or we'll all croak. How many Elders you got now?'

The change of subject—was it a change of subject?—made me hesitate. I thought of the people I'd visited on the way in, of the other middle-aged and elderly people living around the circle of land here. 'Fifty?' That was probably too many but pride stopped me altering the estimate. I ploughed on. 'How can you teach the children, Magda, is it? You aren't trained in what they need.' Rude to say she couldn't read or write, when it was likely the simple truth?

'Your kids don't need what you teach no more,' Albert stated.

I stood, reminding myself that stalking out was not only impolite, it was probably not physically possible for me. 'I don't agree. Daniel, I was hoping to talk to you about persuading some of the isolated groups further out from us to move back, arranging a real town meeting. This is silly. What good would I be wandering around in the bush, particularly when summer comes? Magda, Albert, you'll be

131

Nightsiders   Sue Isle

welcome to attend the regular meeting when the full moon comes; we meet at the Parliament.'

'You're an Elder of your folk. If you talk to these people, they'll listen to you about changes,' said Albert, still calmly, as I made my way to the door.

'My folk! You've got white ancestors as well as Aboriginal. Aren't they both important?'

'Albert's mistaken when he says your children don't need your teaching,' Mag said firmly. 'It's the lessons from the folk before you that they don't need.'

'Are you saying the tribals want to come in to the city land?' I asked, turning at the door. 'Town council will probably agree to that. It's not like we don't do things together. You've taken our children out to teach them about bush tucker, we've helped you with medical care.'

'That's the truth,' Magda agreed and she stood, much more easily than I had. She walked towards me, still talking as though the men weren't even in the room. 'But you got to come out as well. Those folk who hide away, they got to come out, share what they know. Then your kids, they won't be like the old folks, hangin' on at the edge. They'll be something new, something that thrives here.'

'Shani and Itch already are,' I said.

'They need more,' she said. 'They're goin' out, you're huddling in here.'

'I am not huddling!'

'We got the winter to work in,' Mag went on. I opened the door to go out but she slipped out with me. 'That's a start. I figure you can get to the sea, talk with the folks in the caves there.'

132

The Schoolteacher's Tale

'You can do it, better than I can,' I said. 'There isn't another trained teacher, though I'm working with a couple of trainees now. We should have trained people before now but we didn't. It's stupid for me just to take off.'

'You're not taking off,' she said, following down the stairs and quickening her step to draw level with me. I kept a hand on the railing and prayed it wouldn't fall off, so that I wouldn't have to call for the guys to carry me out. 'You're going into your country. Taking the teaching out.'

'Albert said my teaching wasn't needed. Maybe he's right! What have the children got to read but a lot of old books and street signs?'

'You've got more'n that to teach. You remember the old times, the good parts and the bad. If your people aren't to vanish, you got to teach that stuff.'

'George Santayana,' I said. 'Those who cannot remember the past are condemned to repeat it. Is that what you mean?'

I finally reached the bottom of the last flight of stairs. Charisse scrambled up, surprised to see me on my solitary, unassisted feet and startled, I'd swear, to see the other elderly woman beside me. Her stare said it: *Where'd she come from?* I didn't help her. I kept walking. I figured after a few minutes, Mag had given up. I couldn't hear anyone about. I decided I must be headed for the school, or at least my feet were. That was where they were most used to going; home to school, school to market, market to home.

Around the back of the stone monolith that was the state library, a bit crumbly now, was a door leading into a lecture theatre. Now the school. I had candles and lanterns but didn't want to go to the trouble of getting them out. Never

133

Nightsiders   Sue Isle

mind, I'd just go in, sit for a bit and then muster my strength
to walk the ten minutes home.

'Powerful place,' Mag said.

I screeched. I couldn't help it.

'I'm not gonna take it from you, don't worry about that.'

'Just how would you "take" the school anyway?' I
demanded, dropping any pretence at politeness. Right now
I wasn't even sure I liked the woman. She'd been asked to
Shani's wedding but she hadn't been asked into my life and
concerns. 'If you want to stay here and help, that's good,
that's how we live, but please drop the mysticism and wise
pronouncements, would you?'

'Don't mean it like that,' Mag said, unruffled. 'I'm just
not so good at explaining myself, that's all.' She paused for
a few minutes. 'We been through it and under it and over
it a few times; we got to come together more than we have.
Albert and me and some others, we already been around
talking to folk. Years ago, we did. Nyungar who lived in
the city, away from country, they forgot a lot. They didn't
listen to the Elders, and some of them lost who they were.
Children birthing children; you're old enough to remember
those times, right? So we come got them, brought 'em in
with us. Now you got folk out there.' She moved her arm
in a semicircle, looking somewhere beyond the solid stone
wall of the lecture theatre. 'They'll listen to you, not us.
They don't trust us.'

'Nobody trusts anyone not of their tribe, their group,' I
agreed. 'All of us have become very tribal, we don't know
what's happening beyond ourselves. But some of those
people who live separately, like the group I saw when Itch

The Schoolteacher's Tale

and Shani collected me, they aren't the kind of people we necessarily want close at hand. Some people evaded the Evacuation because they didn't want to move, they didn't want to go anywhere unfamiliar. Some evaded it because they were, well, feral.'

'Oh yeah,' Mag muttered, chuckling. 'You got that right, lady.'

'But you don't need me,' I said firmly. 'I don't move very fast, I have bad joints, a bad temper and I like my comforts, few though they are these days. Go ask somebody else.'

'They're kids,' Mag said, just when I thought I'd gotten off a really good last few words. I turned away from the school door in frustration. 'Grown up kids, some of them,' she added as an afterthought. 'They'll listen to a teacher lady, too right they will.'

I headed for home and didn't speak to her again, though she followed for awhile, too damn easily for my pride, repeating her previous arguments as though that would convince me. She dropped away about three quarters of the way, without me noticing; I glanced to where she'd been walking and she wasn't there. Nor could I see her behind me. I continued on past Davy and Jen's silent house to my home.

Three days later it rained. If it was a sign, it was one I didn't understand. I thought of all the tanks around our habitat area, catching and keeping that water. Maybe it was only hope.

There were some children outside my house that evening, probably my students, but they moved away when I came outside. When I retreated in, they came back and watched.

135

The next day, there was no one in school.

By afternoon, I was seriously anxious. I put on my hat and ventured forth, heading first for Alex and Janine's place. I knew they had at least eight children and young teenagers resident. However, Alex was no help when he heard why I had come. 'I thought they went to school,' he said, blinking in the brightness at his doorway. Like most of us, even in the cooler season, he maintained a nocturnal cycle.

'Well, they didn't. No one's there!'

'I'll give them hell when they get back if you want, Ellen, but you know we can't actually tell them what to do. They belong here more than we do.'

I went back to the school for want of a better idea. No one was about in the street and I perspired in the heat even though this day was officially 'cool'. I hoped at least the younger children would come, but what I saw instead, in the shade of the Art Gallery's tall wall was the donkey cart which had carried me to our 'celebrity' teen wedding. Shani was in the driver's seat and Itch stood at the donkey's head.

'What's the occasion?' I demanded, instead of greeting them politely, as I usually tried to do with everyone, no matter their age.

'We're here to take you where you need to go,' Shani said, a little warily.

'Where's that? Did Mag and her nephew tell you to say that?'

Shani blinked and rubbed her eyes. 'They went home. They came back by our house to say they'd talked to you and now they were leaving.'

136

The Schoolteacher's Tale

When she stopped speaking, the world was intensely quiet. Rare for around here, where people congregated, close to the school, our nucleus of learning which was all we had of the world. *Of the old world*, I corrected myself. Shani waited for me. So did Itch and I found myself staring at him, this teenaged Japanese boy, expert scrounger and player of roles, who in this world was a man, as Shani was a woman. Alex's sleepy defence came back to me: 'They belong here more than we do.'

'Just tell me where the children are, why they didn't come to school?'

'Oh,' Itch said and grinned—with relief, I thought. Was I that scary? 'Somebody came through saying they'd found a mob of crabs on the river mud flats, biggest in a long while, and all the kids just took off that way. Don't worry, they probably mean to bring you some, Miss Wakeling.'

I sighed. Paranoia was in full swing. My children weren't on strike. They were doing exactly what the community needed them to do. The waiting air around me was purely my own creation. Then I looked at the teenagers and at Ed, the donkey, who had a back leg cocked in that purely equine way of total relaxation. He flicked his long hairy ears at me.

There were bags on the cart, stowed in the tray behind the driver seat.

I took a long breath. The clear air was unexpectedly delicious. 'We need to stop at my house, for me to pack some things. Then I want you to drive me to the sea. Can you do that?'

'That's why we're here,' Itch said.

***

On the road, picking our way around dead cars and potholes and debris, we found Mag and Albert, with a small group of their people, camped and waiting. Mag said she'd head right in and let the children know what was happening. Albert and the others collected themselves and their kit and followed around us. It didn't feel like anyone's victory, or that I had lost an argument. More like the world had opened up enough to let them in.

About the Author

Sue Isle lives in Perth, Western Australia and would like to be cremated—just not right now—in case anything untoward happens after death. She has read way too much about vampires, werewolves and end of the world scenarios. She works as a court transcriber and has been privy to lots of fascinating information that can never be used in fiction.

Sue has been writing and publishing short stories since the 1980s. Her stories have appeared in publications such as *Aurealis*, *Agog*, *New Ceres Nights*, *Shiny*, *Tales of the Unanticipated*, *Orb* and *Andromeda Spaceways Inflight Magazine*. She has also had two books published, *Scale of Dragon*, *Tooth of Wolf* and *Wolf Children*.

This collection came out of Sue's interest and concern for the subject of climate change, combined with the fact that many sf/horror writers love to destroy their hometown in print. Her other interests include history, environmentalism, attending sf conventions, roleplay gaming and gardening.

Sue lives with a pack of pet rats who are ever appreciative of more paper to rip up. This book is dedicated to them and their little gnashers and then placed high up out of reach.

Twelve Planets

What Are the Twelve Planets?

The Twelve Planets are twelve boutique collections by some of Australia's finest short story writers. Varied across genre and style, each collection will offer four short stories and a unique glimpse into worlds fashioned by some of our favourite storytellers. Each author has taken the brief of 4 stories and up to 40 000 words in their own direction. Some are quartet suites of linked stories. Others are tasters of the range and style of the writer. Each release will bring something unexpected to our subscriber's mailboxes.

When Are the Twelve Planets

The Twelve Planets will spread over 2011 and 2012, with six books released between February and November each year.

The first three titles will be *Nightsiders* by Sue Isle (March), *Love and Romanpunk* by Tansy Rayner Roberts (May) and the third collection will be *Thief of Lives* by Lucy Sussex (July).

How to Receive the Twelve Planets

The Twelve Planets will be available for purchase in several ways:

Single collections will be priced at $20/$23 International each including postage.

A season's pass will offer the three collections of the season for $50/$65 International including postage and each sent out on release, or on purchase of season's pass.

Full subscriptions to the series are $180/$215 International including postage and each sent out on release.

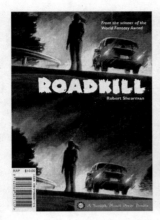

Roadkill *Robert Shearman*

Siren Beat *Tansy Rayner Roberts*

A Twelfth Planet Press Double

Two novelettes—*Roadkill* by Robert Shearman and *Siren Beat* by Tansy Rayner Roberts—published in tête-bêche format form the first Twelfth Planet Press Double.

Roadkill is a squeamishly uncomfortable story with the kind of illicit weekend away that you never want to have.

Siren Beat is a paranormal romance sans vampires or werewolves but featuring a very sexy sea pony. A minor group of man-eating sirens on the docks of Hobart would not normally pose much of a challenge for Nancy, but she is distracted by the reappearance of Nick Cadmus, the man she blames for her sister's death.

Siren Beat
Winner of the WSFA Small Press Short Story Award
Roadkill
Shortlisted for British Fantasy Award for Best Novella

Horn *Peter M. Ball*

There's a dead girl in a dumpster and a unicorn on the loose. No-one knows how bad that combination can get better than Miriam Aster. What starts as a consulting job for city homicide quickly becomes a tangled knot of unexpected questions, and working out the link between the dead girl and the unicorn will draw Aster back into the world of the exiled fey she thought she'd left behind ten years ago.

Dead girls and unicorns? How warped can this get?

Locus Recommended Reading List

Shortlisted for Best Fantasy Novel and Best Horror Novel, Aurealis Awards

Bleed *Peter M. Ball*

For ten years ex-cop Miriam Aster has been living with her one big mistake—agreeing to kill three men for the exiled Queen of Faerie. But when an old case comes back to haunt her it brings a spectre of the past with it, forcing Aster to ally herself with a stuntwoman and a magic cat in order to rescue a kidnapped TV star from the land of Faerie and stop the half-breed sorcerer who needs Aster's blood.

Shortlisted for Australian Shadow Award for Best Long Work

Glitter Rose

Marianne de Pierres

The *Glitter Rose* Collection features five short stories by Marianne de Pierres—four previously published and one new story. Each copy of this limited edition print run is signed and presented in a beautiful hardbound cover, with internal black and white illustrations.

The *Glitter Rose* stories are set against the background of Carmine Island (an island reminiscent of Stradbroke Island, Queensland) where a decade ago spores from deep in the ocean blew in, by a freak of nature, and settled on the island. These spores bring fierce allergies to the inhabitants of the island. And maybe other, more sinister effects. As we follow Tinashi's journey of moving to and settling into island life, we get a clearer picture of just what is happening on Carmine Island.

Sprawl

Sprawl is an exciting new original anthology, glimpsing into the strange, dark, and often wondrous magics that fill the days and nights of Australia's endlessly stretching suburbs.

Liz Argall/Matt Huynh—Seed Dreams (comic)
Peter Ball—One Saturday Night, With Angel
Deborah Biancotti—Never Going Home
Simon Brown—Sweep
Stephanie Campisi—How to Select a Durian at Footscray Market
Thoraiya Dyer—Yowie
Dirk Flinthart—Walker
Paul Haines—Her Gallant Needs
L L Hannett—Weightless
Pete Kempshall—Signature Walk
Ben Peek—White Crocodile Jazz
Tansy Rayner Roberts—Relentless Adaptations
Barbara Robson—Neighbourhood Watch
Angela Slatter—Brisneyland by Night
Cat Sparks—All The Love in the World
Anna Tambour—Gnawer of the Moon Seeks Summit of Paradise
Kaaron Warren—Loss
Sean Williams—Parched (poem)

Locus Recommended Reading List